Centennial:
South Euclid 1917-2017

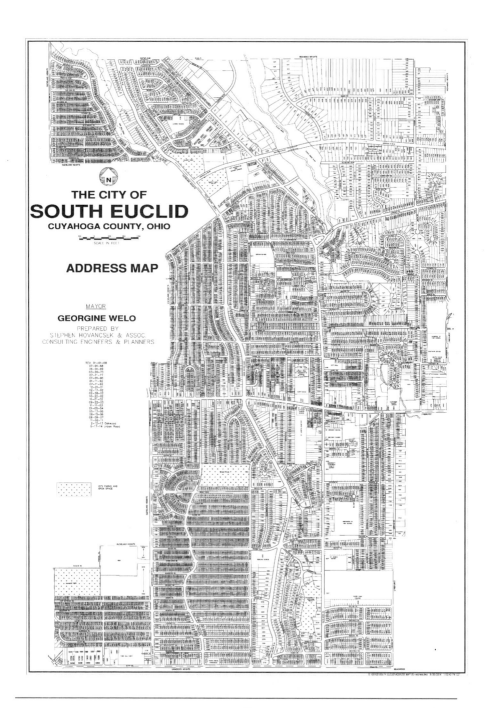

THE CITY OF
SOUTH EUCLID
CUYAHOGA COUNTY, OHIO

SCALE IN FEET

ADDRESS MAP

MAYOR

GEORGINE WELO

PREPARED BY
STEPHEN HOVANCSEK & ASSOC.
CONSULTING ENGINEERS & PLANNERS

Centennial:
South Euclid 1917-2017

Edited by:

Eileen Quinlan, SND, PhD

Robert McKimm

South Euclid – Lyndhurst Historical Society Publications

2017

First Printing: 2017

ISBN: 978-0-692-88938-1

Library of Congress No. 2017907276

South Euclid – Lyndhurst Historical Society Publications
4629 Mayfield Road
South Euclid, OH 44121

www.SE-Lhistory.org

Special discounts are available on quantity purchases by corporations, associations, educators, and others. For details, contact the publisher at the above listed address.

U.S. trade bookstores and wholesalers: Please contact South Euclid – Lyndhurst Historical Society Tel: (216) 970-2333 or email info@SE-Lhistory.org

Dedication

To all the people who have particated in South Euclid's
journey before and during these 100 years.

Contents

Acknowledgements.. ix

Foreword.. x

Preface xi

Introduction.. 1

A Million Feet Above South Euclid 5

The Man in the Mansion.. 21

The Miller and Broome Families... 25

Memories of Childhood around 1950................................... 31

A Teenager in the 1970s... 33

Survival on the Playground Slide 39

The Welos.. 43

South Euclid on the Portage Escarpment:
    Forces of Landscape Change 49

Our First Visitors: American Indians 67

South Euclid in the Western Reserve:
    The Legacy of Euclid Township.................................. 73

Euclid Creek Reservation and
    the Civilian Conservation Corps................................. 81

Notre Dame College 93

The City Incinerator... 107

Cedar Center in the 1940s - 1950s...................................... 109

Maymore Shopping Center.. 113

The Story of Warehouse Beverage 117

Gentlemen's Grooming Barbershop 121

Our Recycling Committee 123

Our Historical Society.. 127

The Blossoming of the Garden Club 131

The First Baptist Church of South Euclid (FBCSE)...................... 135

The Doll House... 137

Notes 141

References... 147

Acknowledgements

We would like to thank our authors, each and every one, but especially those who were individually asked if they would produce specific essays, namely Richard A. Barone for the Telling essay, Dr. Roy Larick from the Euclid Historical Society for the geology and surveying essays, Rebecca Jones Macko for the American Indian essay, Sally Accorti Martin for the Welo essay, Laura Peskin of the Euclid Historical Society for the Euclid Creek CCC essay, Dr. Eileen Quinlan SND for the essay on Notre Dame College (as well as her massive help in editing this publication), and Carl Walz for recounting his adventures here and in space.

ILLUSTRATIONS

Cover and elsewhere centennial logos used by permission from the city of South Euclid. Pages 5,13,16 astronaut photos from NASA; 21,Telling Mansion, South Euclid – Lyndhurst Historical Society[SELHS]; 40, Adrian Slide, Robert McKimm[RMcK]; 43, Welos in 2015 Memorial Day Parade, photo provided by City of South Euclid; 49-66 geology captions and credits in Notes Section; 67, Hopewell, furnished by National Park Service; 73-80, Legacy of Township, captions and credits in Notes Section; 81, Euclid Creek 1930 map, Cleveland Metroparks[CMP]; 86, Bert Lange drawing of Camp Euclid from Camp Euclid Surveyor 3/29/1937; 86, Euclid Creek Shale Welsh Woods CCC wall remnant, Laura Peskin; 88, CCC tree planting, [SELHS]; 91, Welsh Woods 1940, Euclid Historical Society; 95, Administration Bldg., Notre Dame College Archives, [NDC], 103 Art in the Circle 2012, [NDC]; 105 aerial views, [NDC]; 109, Cedar Center 1930s, [SELHS]; 113 Store from Carole Prochaska Smith; 114, Maymore, [RMcK]; 117, Original Store from Speyer Family[SP]; 118, Beverage Store, [SP]; 121, logo from Shironda Williams; 123, Parade Banner furnished by SERC; 127, Helen Urban, [SELHS]; 128, Charter Members, [SELHS]; 134, group photo furnished by Garden Club; 135, church, [RMcK]; 137&138, house by Dale Ann Guidroz-Henderson.

Foreword

At the swearing-in ceremony, when I was newly elected to South Euclid City Council, I was given a copy of the *Golden Jubilee 1917-1967 South Euclid*, a book of the proud heritage of our community, written by the Golden Jubilee Book Committee. That book is valuable for its many documented historical facts about South Euclid's founding, settlement and growth. I diligently read the book and learned quickly about the great, rich history of the city I now served and now, some twenty-five years later, I have not forgotten the Golden Jubilee Book Committee.

When I examine the essays submitted for this centennial book, I find rich deposits of gold. Each author has attempted to capture one life or time in South Euclid. Each one holds a sense of pride as the author gives the story a special "twist," as though putting a spin on a ball. Today, fifty years later, the Centennial Book committee has used its vigor to inspire those who live or have lived in South Euclid to set down a historical record that will be treasured.

The reader will soon discover that these essays and stories are in an easy-reading form, with each independent writer allowing every line to reveal personal memories or views. You can feel that they really put their hearts and souls into their compositions. What I enjoyed most was that they brought back memories of people, places and times that were friendly and sometimes funny.

There you have it: this centennial book is a short, valuable collection of essays written by local individuals who, fifty years later, chose to present an entertaining history of our city. I would like to thank the South Euclid Historical Society, the Centennial Committee and all the authors who have contributed to make this commemorative publication.

Georgine Welo, Mayor of South Euclid

Preface

1917 was a challenging year, here and for the world as a whole. The "Great War," also known as "The War to End All Wars," had begun in Europe in 1914 and during 1917 the United States joined in.

Locally a failed school levy caused the Township Board to decide to close the Euclidville School (Euclidville was renamed Lyndhurst in 1921 and the school is the Little Red Schoolhouse now moved behind the SE-L Schools Administration Building). Euclidville discovered that, if they incorporated as a village, they could control their own school system. They did so. They then also controlled the schools of adjacent unincorporated locales, so both South Euclid and Claribel (now named Richmond Heights)) incorporated within a few months in defense. So, 2017 is the centennial of all three cities.

The SE-L Historical Society thought a book celebrating all three cities centennials would be appropriate. We approached all three cities and none were particularly interested in such a book. South Euclid, though, wanted a book for just their centennial. They had a book written for the first 50 years. It has no author of record. In 2000 Nancy Schuemann wrote a sequel taking our history to 2000. South Euclid's initial thought was a book stretching from there to 2017. We weren't interested. Plus, these two books focused on city administrations, and were thus of great interest to city administrators, and some few others. We wanted a book of all the people, places, and things in South Euclid that folks chose to write about. We made an open call for essays and solicited some others. Here are the results.

Bob McKimm, spokesman for the SE-L Historical Society.

Introduction

There was no clear path to organizing these many essays but we grouped them into three basic sections: People; Pre-history and Early History; Places and Things. There's a lot of overlap in these sections and by no means do we even recommend reading them in book order. Just jump in wherever you want.

PEOPLE

A Million Feet Above South Euclid. When the Centennial Committee first met and the topic of "favorite sons and daughters" came up, one name was presented: Carl Walz. He brought us to international fame when he became the man to have then spent the longest time in space—over six months on the International Space Station. He credits his South Euclid childhood and education for starting him on this path.

The Man in the Mansion. Richard A. Barone, whose charitable foundation bought the Telling Mansion, was the logical person to write about William Telling and his mansion on Mayfield.

The Miller and Broome Families. They moved here just prior to the start of World War II and have stayed since.

Memories of Childhood around 1950. Before the 1970s, neighborhoods here were highly segregated by nationality and religion. Outsiders were made to feel unwelcome. Since then the city has become more of a melting pot.

A Teenager in the 1970s. South Euclid's building boom emanated from the baby boom post-WWII. These children were mostly upper grades or 20s in the 1970s.

Survival on the Playground Slide. Jay Haarburger survived strangulation with a little help from his friends.

The Welos. We identified some "favorite sons" but where were our favorite daughters? A moment's thought focused on our first female and current mayor who quickly adopted South Euclid even though she didn't spend her childhood here. It seemed inappropriate to ask her to write her own story so we asked Sally Martin, our housing manager, since we were most impressed by the writing quality in many of her "SEL Experience" columns. Herein are the results.

PREHISTORY AND EARLY HISTORY

South Euclid on the Portage Escarpment: Forces of Landscape Change. Any history of South Euclid is incomplete without a mention of the topography and rock layers below. Quarrying represented much of our early economy and streams supplied water to the many farmlands. Dr. Roy Larick, Vice-President of the Euclid Historical Society wrote this in-depth essay of the history and geology suitable for anything from a quick perusal to serious study.

Our First Visitors: The American Indians. Rebecca Jones Macko, a National Park Service Interpretive Ranger at our Cuyahoga Valley National Park, has studied the histories of Native American tribes in Ohio and provided this tale of activity in our area.

South Euclid in the Western Reserve: The Legacy of Euclid Township. Dr. Larick is also author of *Euclid Township, 1796-1801: Protest in the Western Reserve.* It summarizes the story of Moses Cleaveland's surveyors herculean task in surveying this region and the renegotiation that ended with their options to get discounted land in a township of their choosing. Ours!

PLACES & THINGS

South Euclid, Euclid Creek Reservation and the Civilian Conservation Corps. Author Laura Peskin wrote this history of Euclid Creek Metropark and the CCC camp that helped build it.

Notre Dame College. Eileen Quinlan, a Sister of Notre Dame and English Professor wrote this essay about her school.

The City Incinerator. When Janet Dreyer bought her home she didn't know her neighbor was the city's incinerator.

Cedar Center in the 1940s – 1950s. Charles Lissauer reminisces about the early days of Cedar Center.

Maymore Shopping Center. Carole Prochaska Smith tells the tale of the business started by her father-in-law and the rental properties they acquired.

The Story of Warehouse Beverage. Three members of the Speyer family reveal their father's legacy.

Gentlemen's Grooming Barbershop. This barbershop is a recent transplant to South Euclid.

Our Recycling Committee. Their growth from a few bins to curbside recycling and periodic drives.

Our Historical Society. This was almost omitted because we had to write it instead of just editing it. And items like this book speak for themselves. But we want you to know the less obvious activities of our organization.

The Blossoming of the Garden Club. The history walk down Green Road is not complete without pausing at Sue Gold's home and admiring the talents

The First Baptist Church of South Euclid (FBCSE). The church pastor tells of this church's history.

The Doll House. Dale Ann's home on Golfway garnered the nickname "The Doll House."

A Million Feet Above South Euclid

By Carl Walz

When I stop to think about the influence of South Euclid on my life, I am amazed at the many impacts! From the parks to schools, from sports to education, South Euclid had many significant influences on my future. South Euclid was a big part of my growing up, the friends and activities I participated in, my education, interest in music, and eventually my wife and family.

My growing up was all in South Euclid and Lyndhurst. My earliest memories come from our family home at the corner of Mayfield and Belvoir. We lived there for 15 years, and I had a wonderful childhood. I was able to walk to school, first to Victory Park for Kindergarten, and then to St. Gregory's School, where I spent grades 1 through 8. I recall playing in my backyard, which backed up to Petronzio Landscaping and Mayfair Monuments. My brother John and I would use the discarded wooden shipping crates from the monuments to build forts in our backyard.

John and I were paper carriers for the Cleveland Press, with a route that included Westdale, Laclede, Belvoir, and Wrenford Roads. Carrying the papers was a fun job that allowed my brother and me to meet other paper carriers. We also got a chance to meet our neighbors, especially when we collected for the route. The paper route was often challenging in the winter, when we would have to trudge through the snow to deliver the newspapers, but we would meet neighbors who would need their driveways shoveled, and that gave John and me a chance to make extra money.

Westdale was a great road to live on because it was just down the street from Bexley Park. I played baseball (organized and pick-up games), and swam at the pool there. I recall swimming lessons on summer mornings when temperatures in the low 60's would make for some brisk lessons! Living on Westdale allowed us to have perfect seats for the South Euclid Homeday parades. With my mom and dad, my sisters Lu Anne and Kathy, and my brother John, I watched fire trucks, marching bands, and dignitaries pass by our house on the way to the Park for the festivities. One of the dignitaries I remember was the mayor, George Urban, who always had little girls in the car with him as he drove by. Many years later at Brush High School, I would meet one of those girls, Pam Glady, one of Mayor Urban's granddaughters. Pam and I eventually dated, and were married in South Euclid at St. Gregory's in 1976.

I always enjoyed the walk to school, passing by many interesting shops on the way to and from school. Passing by Damon's candies, John and I occasionally stopped in to spend some of our paper route money on their fine confections. We would walk by Warehouse

Beverage (it's still there!), and sometimes stop for a cold Pepsi or Coke. Walking home from school in the late spring would take us past Crème-O-Freeze, a great gathering spot for after-baseball treats! We'd purchase necessities at South Euclid Hardware and the May-Green Drugstore. On the way to school we would typically cross Green Road protected by Cliff Hoffman of the South Euclid Police. Cliff always referred to us as "grasshoppers" as we crossed, which always struck me as a fun name! (Cliff and my uncle Mo Chandler had served in the Marines together during World War II.)

I was fortunate to get a great education while growing up in South Euclid. At St. Gregory the Great school, each grade had 3 classes, each class with 35-40 students. Our teachers were Sisters of Notre Dame and lay teachers, very dedicated teachers who were able to handle large classes full of boisterous students. We were the baby boomer generation, so there were a lot of kids! One of my strongest memories was watching the early astronaut launches in our classrooms. Remote classroom instruction was in its infancy, and we had black and white televisions that were used for lessons as well as showing the countdowns and launches. I remember watching several of the Project Mercury and Gemini launches and splashdowns while at St. Greg's. I think that early exposure to space flight, and the fact that John Glenn was an Ohioan and the first American to orbit the Earth, made a deep impression that led me to seek a future in aerospace!

When I was an 8th grader, our family moved a short way from Westdale to a new community off Whitehall and Green Roads. After graduation from St. Greg's, I switched to public school, with a new walking route along Dorsh Road to Memorial Junior High, where I attended 9th grade. Going to Memorial was a big change from St. Gregory, without the religious aspect and with the need to change classroom and teachers. Several of my friends from St. Gregory made the change to public school in 9th grade as well, and I also had a chance to meet many new friends. I was very involved in sports at Memorial, playing football, baseball, and wrestling. This was my first experience with highly organized athletic teams and it was very exciting. On Friday nights, Brush High School was the destination for the senior high sports experience. Our Memorial group sat together for Brush football and basketball games.

Moving from Memorial to Brush in 10th grade was a huge jump. The school was much larger, and the students were much bigger! My Brush teachers were highly experienced and brought great depth to the classes they taught. At Brush, I joined the mixed chorus, and met a number of lifelong friends. In choir, we had kids from both Memorial and Greenview, so I got to know the Greenview kids much better. Mr. Lindley Hall was a great music teacher who inspired us to perform at the highest levels. As I advanced at Brush, as our choir sang ever more difficult pieces, we performed them extremely well. From chorus, I became involved in a number of singing groups, including "The Fabulous Blue Moons" which specialized in music of the 1950's and 60's, and which continues playing in the Cleveland area to this day. I became exposed to music competitions and had the chance to participate in a musical, The Music Man.

The Music Man was a great experience which brought me in contact with other notable teachers, Mrs. Dorothy Herron and Ms. Candy Clemson. Mrs. Herron worked with us on our dialogue, and became a friend and great mentor. In her British Literature classes the works of British authors came alive. Her excellent instruction allowed me to take advanced English classes when I started college at John Carroll. Ms. Clemson was a gifted and dedicated art teacher who worked closely with us on art and costumes. It seemed like she lived at

Brush during the preparation for The Music Man. Her presence helped us all in the hectic times during the final rehearsals and the performances. Ms. Clemson also worked with "The Fabulous Blue Moons" to develop our costumes and our "look."

I had always been interested in science at St. Gregory's and that interest continued as I moved on to Brush. Of my excellent science teachers, Mr. Al Eich, my physics teacher, had the greatest impact on my future professional life. Mr. Eich used a college physics textbook and his attention to detail allowed us to understand complex ideas. I had originally thought that I would study medicine but Mr. Eich inspired me to pursue physics. I earned bachelor's and master's degrees in physics from Kent State and John Carroll, respectively, and my first job in the Air Force was in a radiation laboratory. My physics degree led to my selection for the highly competitive Air Force Test Pilot School, which provided a new professional opportunity in aerospace and led to my selection for the astronaut office in 1990.

Fast forward to 1993, when I was assigned to my first space flight, STS-51, the 17th flight of the Space Shuttle Discovery. The STS-51 crew consisted of me, commander Frank Culbertson, pilot Bill Ready, and mission specialists Jim Newman and Dan Bursch. (Jim, Dan and I were members for the 13th astronaut class selected in 1990.) Our mission was to deploy the Advanced Communications Technology Satellite (ACTS), a satellite communications test bed developed by Cleveland's Lewis (now Glenn) Research Center. The ACTS was paired with the second flight of Orbital Science's Transfer Orbit Stage to propel the ACTS into its place in geostationary orbit. The STS-51 flight also included a second satellite, the Astro Shuttle Pallet Satellite (Astro-SPAS) a German-developed ultra-violet telescope, which was deployed using the shuttle robotic arm. Our planned launch date was July 17, 1993, and the original plan had us deploying ACTS on Flight

Day 1, at the end of launch day, and AstroSPAS on the second flight day. As our training progressed, a spacewalk was added to the planned activities, with Jim Newman and me scheduled to step outside the Discovery. Our crew would also perform several crew-developed experiments, a GPS test in space, and a system that could display selected shuttle data not usually accessible to the crew.

Our scheduled launch day in July was a beautiful blue morning. We had our breakfast, suited up, and strapped into the Discovery. The countdown proceeded to T-20 minutes, and then held as the engineers tried to clear a fault with the launch pad separation bolts that release the shuttle after engine start. Unfortunately, the fault never cleared, and the launch was scrubbed. We unstrapped from the shuttle and flew back to Houston while the fault was resolved. A week later, on July 24th, we were ready again. On another beautiful day, we woke up, had breakfast, suited up, strapped into Discovery, and got ready for launch. The countdown continued past 20 minutes, past the 1 minute point, then stopped at 19 seconds, when another fault appeared. One of the hydraulic systems that provide steering power to the space shuttle booster rockets, essential to a safe launch, failed to start. So we unstrapped from the shuttle again, flew back to Houston, and waited while the fault was resolved. In the process of setting a new launch date, NASA had to delay again to avoid a meteor shower. Our launch date was reset for August 12. We again awoke to a beautiful blue morning, had breakfast, suited up, and strapped in for the third time. The countdown proceeded down past 20 minutes, past 19 seconds, down past 6 seconds when the space shuttle engines came to life with a roar and enormous shaking . . . only to shut down at 3 seconds prior to launch! Once we were told the launch pad was safe, we unstrapped from the space shuttle, flew back to Houston, and took a vacation. We had at least a month's delay while the main engines were removed and replaced on the launch pad.

After the shuttle engines had been replaced, our crew flew back to Florida in September to try to launch again. On the morning of September 12, the crew awoke to a beautiful clear Florida morning. The weather was clear, and we had our crew breakfast, suited up, drove to the launch pad, rode the elevator to the 195 ft. level, and strapped into Discovery for the fourth time. The countdown proceeded passed 20 minutes, passed 19 seconds, the engines started and stayed lit - and at T-0, the solid rockets ignited, and the space shuttle leapt off the launch pad. As we began the ascent, the vibration in the space shuttle cabin was incredible. As we accelerated through the atmosphere, we could feel and hear the air, and were pushed down into our seats so that we felt three times heavier than normal! We rode the solid rocket motors for two minutes until they ran out of fuel and separated from the rest of the shuttle with a loud BANG! Instantly, we went back to one "g". We then continued on the space shuttle main engines, accelerating again, but with a much less noisy ride. Shortly after that, we were back at three "g" and on our way to orbit. Eight minutes and thirty seconds after launch, the space shuttle main engines shut down, and we were in orbit and instantly weightless! Everything around me started floating, and as I unstrapped from my seat, I was floating as well! It was amazing.

From the Discovery's mid-deck I floated to the flight deck and began taking photographs of our now-detached external fuel tank, the "ET", which rode with us to orbit. As I was taking pictures, I saw the beautiful Earth below, with the blue Atlantic ocean as a backdrop for the large, charred orange tank. After we moved away from the ET, we began the rest of flight day one, adjusting our orbital altitude, opening our payload bay doors, and getting ready to deploy our first satellite, the ACTS, on our fifth orbit. We communicated with Mission Control using relay satellites. In the shuttle payload bay, we had to open a large mechanical cradle, elevate the satellite and its transfer orbit stage (TOS) in the payload bay, and verify commanding from the shuttle to the satellite. As we were verifying commanding, we realized that we had lost voice communication with Earth. As time ticked by toward the planned deployment, we knew that we would not be able to deploy as planned. We ran through our communications malfunction checklist to reestablish communications and successfully reconnected with mission control. Our flight control team had been thinking the same way we were, and came up with a new deployment time on the next orbit. That took the deployment into our sleep preparation period, but we gladly continued the deployment checklist.

On that next orbit, with communications reestablished, we finished the deployment checklist, and I toggled the switch to fire the separation explosives to release the ACTS and its transfer orbit stage from the shuttle. The ACTS gracefully glided over the shuttle crew compartment as we photographed and videotaped the spacecraft motion. Around the satellite, a halo of unknown material floated radially away from the aft portion of the payload bay. As the ACTS continued to move away, we gently maneuvered the shuttle away and turned our shuttle heat shield toward the satellite. We moved our robotic arm's cameras to a position from which we could view the ignition of the transfer orbit stage, and waited for the TOS engine to ignite. The engine did light as planned, and the ACTS was lifted successfully into its place in geostationary orbit. We then set up our cameras to downlink the video and got ready for sleep after our very eventful launch day.

During the night, Mission Control reviewed our downlinked video and discovered that the halo of debris was indeed something not expected during the deployment. During operations the next morning, as we removed the Astro-SPAS payload from Discovery's payload bay with the shuttle robotic arm, we saw a highly-damaged deployment cradle which clearly was the source of the debris that escaped during  the deployment. In addition, there was a discolored brown ring on the normally-white aft bulkhead where explosive gases had escaped during deployment. The deployment cradle looked like a can with the lid partially opened! As the mission continued, we continued our flight plan, completing a spacewalk, several experiments, and IMAX filming of the Earth and the Astro-SPAS. On the ground, engineers and flight controllers looked at pictures of the cradle and decided that the damaged cradle did not pose a threat to Discovery during reentry and landing. After nearly 10 days in orbit, we retrieved the Astro-SPAS satellite, closed the payload bay doors and returned to Kennedy Space Center, performing the first nighttime landing at the Shuttle Landing Facility there.

While training for my STS-51 flight, I was assigned to my second flight, the STS-65, called the Second International Microgravity Flight, the 17th flight of the space shuttle Columbia. Instead of having two satellites in the payload bay, we had a large pressurized laboratory— the Spacelab, which held over 80 experiments from the U.S, Europe, Canada, and Japan. Commander Bob Cabana, pilot Jim Halsell, and I were assigned about a year prior to the flight, and joined a payload team that had been already training for a year: Rick Hieb, Leroy Chiao, Don Thomas, and Chiaki Mukai, the first Japanese woman to fly in space.

Don Thomas, on his first flight, was a Cleveland Heights High School and Case grad. Jim, Leroy, and Don were all my astronaut classmates.

Unlike the STS-51 flight, the STS-65 had only one countdown. On the morning of July 8th, 1994, under a beautiful blue sky, the countdown proceeded on schedule without issue. At T-6 seconds, the shuttle main engines ignited—and stayed lit! At T-0 seconds, the solid rocket boosters ignited, the exploding bolts released us from the launch pad, and we lifted skyward and into orbit. On STS-65 I was the flight engineer, sitting with the commander and pilot on the flight deck where I was able to see out the forward windows, and also to look up at the windows on the ceiling of the crew compartment. As we accelerated into space, my focus was primarily on the gauges and displays in front of me, but I did have a chance to glance over my head to see Kennedy Space Center receding from view and the Atlantic Ocean coming into view. I saw and heard the separation rockets as they pushed the expended boosters away with a bang and a flash. As we continued to orbit, the familiar g-forces during ascent grew to three g's. What was new during this ascent was the view of Earth and the flashes of light as the plume from the shuttle main engines curled around the space shuttle.

Once in orbit, we turned the space shuttle from a space transportation system to a state-of-the art laboratory. The Spacelab was connected to the shuttle crew compartment by a long tunnel that allowed us to float effortlessly from the shuttle mid-deck to the lab, where the science team conducted the life and physical science experiments that would be the focus of our two-week mission. My job on this flight was to maintain Columbia in tip-top operating shape so that all our science objectives could be completed. The science mission included the Space Acceleration Measurement System (SAMS) from

Glenn (then Lewis) Research Center. We operated the laboratory around the clock, with two shifts, red and blue. Don, Leroy and I were on the blue shift, with the rest of the crew on the red shift. During shift handovers, we would share a meal (breakfast for one shift, dinner for the other).

After 14 days, we closed up the Spacelab, turning the space laboratory into a spacecraft again, closed the payload bay doors, and began preparations for reentry. Being on the flight deck during the night allowed a great view of the fire of reentry around Columbia as we entered the atmosphere at Mach 25, that's 25 times the speed of sound. We saw tubes of highly-heated, ionized gas shoot this way and that around the crew compartment, a flashing light on the shuttle flight deck. Ahead of us was a bright fog of ionized gas, first white and then turning pink as we descended into the atmosphere. Shortly after the pink glow, nighttime turned into day as we streaked toward Kennedy Space Center. Soon after that, we crossed Florida, flew over the KSC at 50,000 feet, gracefully turned the gliding shuttle to line up the runway and landed after a very successful 14-day, 17-hour mission.

I flew another space shuttle mission on the space shuttle Atlantis, STS-79, providing supplies to the Russian space station Mir, bringing John Blaha to Mir for his long-duration mission, picking up Shannon Lucid from her record setting stay on Mir, and conducting a number of science experiments and technology demonstrations. That very successful flight led to my selection and training for my 196-day flight on the fourth crew of the International Space Station. This spacecraft circumnavigates the earth about every 90 minutes in a spiral pattern that covers all parts of our globe. Its altitude is nearly 250 miles or over a million feet above the earth.

My time on the International Space Station was an amazing experience. I had been training for more than 4 years for this flight. We were the 4th crew to live on the station, launching on December 5, 2001 from Kennedy Space Center on the Space Shuttle Endeavour, flight STS-108. Two days after launching, we rendezvoused and docked with the Station. Upon arriving, we floated from the shuttle to the station, and within a short period of time, went from shuttle crew members to station crew members. The shuttle flight, in addition to transporting me, Dan Bursch, and our Russian commander Yuri Onufrienko, was primarily a logistic flight, and we spent most of the docked time moving equipment from the shuttle's Multipurpose Logistics Module to the ISS. And NASA had allowed me to bring a music keyboard along to help occupy our brief idle moments.

When Endeavour undocked from the ISS ten days later, it was a strange feeling to watch our transportation from Earth leaving without us as we began what we thought was a 160-day mission. We conducted experiments, maintained the station in tip-top operating condition, and continued the work of assembling the station. We performed biological experiments, physical science experiments, and of course biomedical experiments, in which the crew were the subjects. We performed studies measuring changes in our reflexes from living in microgravity, as well as studies of changes in our lung function. We also had plant and cell experiments, again to

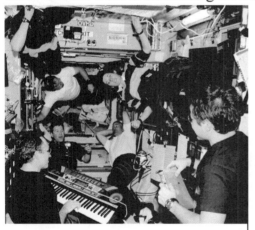

Rare relaxation time

study how organisms grow and mature in space.

The reflex experiment involved sending a steadily increasing jolt of electricity through our legs, generating a reflex kick by the leg. Lung function experiments involved blowing all the air out of our lungs to determine the vital capacity of our lungs. We performed the experiment every month and before and after spacewalks. Our crew performed a total of three spacewalks, two in the Russian Orlan spacesuit and one in the US spacesuit.

Most days we woke up at the same time, around midnight Houston time. We would receive our daily briefing to discuss our plans for the day, and begin our work. Usually we would exercise two hours a day. We would spend about 45 minutes on a treadmill, followed by about 45 minutes of resistance exercise, using elastic bands instead of weights. We would perform work for the Russian segment early in the day, when the Russian specialists were available, and work for the US segment later in the day, when our full US team was available.

Because we had a mixed US/Russian crew, we had both Russian and US food to eat. We really liked having the variety of Russian food, which was very different from the US entrees. I surprised myself by enjoying cans of jellied fish—something normally eaten in Russia but rarely eaten in the US.

We had a number of visitors to the ISS during our flight. The STS-110 crew arrived on the space shuttle Atlantis on April 10, 2002, bringing their crew of seven and the S0 truss, the first element of the station's external truss to provide the structure for the electrical system for the completed station. Atlantis brought our first visitors since the STS-108 crew had departed four months earlier. It was great to see the STS-110 team and work with them to complete our joint task of attaching and activating the huge truss element. They stayed with us for seven days, departing on April 17th. Our second set of visitors came on a Russian Soyuz replacement flight. The Soyuz was a crew capsule used both for transporting crews and as a lifeboat. During our time on the station, the Soyuz was primarily a lifeboat, but it had a limited time allowable on orbit before it had to be replaced. The Soyuz TM-34 flight arrived on April 27, with the Soyuz crew returning in the Soyuz TM-33 spacecraft that had served as our lifeboat for 193 days. The TM crew included Yuri Gidzenko from the first ISS crew, Roberto Vittori from Italy, and the second space tourist, Mark Shuttleworth from South Africa. Soyuz TM-33 undocked and reentered on May 5, 2002.

Our 160-day mission become a 190+ day mission when we were told that our return shuttle flight had been delayed by approximately six weeks due to a failure on the station's robotic arm, which required loading a replacement part onto the shuttle and training the crew in its installation. We took the news in stride. The delay would give Dan and me the US record for the longest US space mission, a record previously held by Shannon Lucid during her spaceflight to the Russian Mir space station.

Our return flight was also on the Space Shuttle Endeavour, STS-111. Launching on June 5, 2002, the flight docked with the ISS on June 7, bringing our replacement crew, Expedition 5, a logistics module, and the Mobile Base System, which would allow the station robotic arm to move along the newly installed S0 truss. I assisted astronaut Peggy Whitson in installing the MBS onto the Mobile Transporter using that very same robotic arm. We unloaded the logistics module and reloaded it with returning science cargo as well as many items that just didn't fit in the limited volume of the station. When the time came to leave the station, it was with mixed feelings. I knew that this would be my last flight to space. I would no longer float freely in space, effortlessly moving from one place to another. I would never again have the fantastic view of the Earth that I enjoyed for more than half a year! But I would be rejoining my family on Earth, seeing my wife Pam again, and sharing in my son's final year in high school and my daughter's final year in college.

Endeavour departed the station on June 15, 2002. Our reentry planned for June 17 was delayed by weather in Florida. We tried again to reenter on the 18th, but without success as the rainy weather continued. Finally, on June 19, with rain again in Florida, we changed our landing destination to Edwards Air Force base in California. Edwards was the place I saw my first space shuttle back in 1983, so it was an appropriate place to close out a space flight career.

It was with great pride that I was able to fly items on the Space Shuttle for the city of South Euclid, my hometown, and St. Gregory and Brush High School. I owe much to South Euclid! Congratulations on your 100th anniversary and I look forward to a very bright future!

Centennial

The Man in the Mansion

By Richard A. Barone

I saw the Telling Mansion for the first time in 1949 when I was in second grade attending Green Road School, which was located just north of Mayfield Road on the east side of Green Road. On this particular day in late spring my mother informed me she would be a little late picking me up at school, so I decided to do a little exploring on my own. As I walked east on Mayfield I came upon a magnificent structure–a mansion–the very kind of thing one would imagine the Wizard of Oz might call home.

Because I grew up in South Euclid, I had explored every inch of the city by the time I was 10 or 11. My father owned a small building supply company at Green and Monticello, and during the summer months I would ride my bicycle from there to the Cleveland Trust bank branch on Mayfield, carrying checks to deposit in his business account. Unless I was in a rush, I found a way to have the Telling Mansion on my route, and a roundabout of the structure was always inspiring. In 1952 when it became a branch of the Cuyahoga County Library system, I would sometimes take a walk through just to assure myself that the smartest people in the city knew who I was.

The 1950s were a wonderful time of growth in the city. New streets were being built, retail stores were springing up along Mayfield Road, and the Mayfield Theater was packed every Saturday afternoon with young moviegoers – 10 cents to get in, 10 cents for popcorn and 5 cents for a candy bar. The city was changing and prospering. As residents settled into their homesteads for the long run, the Telling Mansion became a constant and a familiar source of pride for the community. For a young and growing city, we had the most unique and impressive branch of the entire library system.

Unless you happened to have been one of the older residents in the 1950s, the existence of Mr. Telling and his business interests were all but forgotten. Telling had finished building the mansion in 1928 at the age of 58, just a year before the stock market crash. By the time of his death in 1938, he had lost most of his fortune. Although he had decided to build on the property which had been in his family for generations, he was never able to fully share it with his children and grandchildren. By the time the library system bought it in 1951, it had been through several owners and several uses, including a residence for war brides in the 1940s.

Industrious and frugal in his youth late in the 19th century, Telling launched his career at the age of 23 when he purchased a milk route for the sum of $1,000. Two years later, when it was evident that he was getting nowhere, he and his brother opened an ice cream shop on Euclid Avenue across from Lakeview Cemetery. From these humble beginnings, the Telling empire grew into a major dairy operation. In 1916, the Telling Dairy merged with others forming the Telling Belle Vernon Dairy, becoming one of the largest dairy businesses in Ohio. By the mid-1920s the Telling Belle Vernon Dairy merged into the National Dairy Company where his milk and other dairy products received the Sealtest Seal of Approval.

I never thought the Cuyahoga County Library would ever sell the Telling Mansion, and never imagined that I would ever own it. Like most of the residents of South Euclid, present and past, I wanted it to remain a library and a source of pride for the community. But I, too, was on a mission. I needed to find a home for a national museum which I conceived and funded, the Museum of American Porcelain Art. For most of the 20th century the United States was the world's premier producer of porcelain art. These porcelains adorn such places as the Smithsonian, the White House, and New York's Metropolitan Museum of Art, as well as Buckingham Palace. One of the Vatican's eleven libraries contains only Boehm Porcelain from the United States.

While Dalton, Lladro, Moorecroft, Ardmore and others continue to flourish in distant places, American Porcelain companies such as Boehm, Cybis and Ispanky have closed their doors. This was not due to a lack of talent but because of poor business practices. Artists often lack business skills. Several years ago, I purchased the Boehm Porcelain Company after it had closed its doors. With it came a wealth of archival materials including photographs of most modern-day US Presidents presenting Boehm porcelains to other heads of state.

Like Mr. Telling, Edward Marshall Boehm was a titan in his own right. Both men shared a passion for birds. The Telling Mansion property once contained aviaries second to none in Ohio. Boehm too had aviaries on his property which inspired him to create some of the most beautiful wildlife porcelains in the world. The Museum of American Porcelain Art will bring together the best of these two titans in a national showcase representing the best examples of architecture and art from a time when American ingenuity and perseverance inspired the world.

Centennial

The Miller and Broome Families

By Carole Broome

The Broome/Miller tribe has had a continuing presence in South Euclid since 1941. Four generations have owned four houses in the city and three of those generations are still in residence in two homes. The way we got to this place is a story like so many others: the right place and time and desire to own a house and here we are, seventy-five years later.

It was 1940 when my parents Mort and Bess Miller were in the position to buy their first home, having been renters in East Cleveland and Cleveland Heights since their marriage in 1928. They began looking in those two communities, but an empty lot came up for sale on Plainfield Road. It was in South Euclid but close to Cleveland Heights where my Dad's family had a lot of history as well. They hadn't intended to build a house but they did. So it was that in November of 1941, on the day before Thanksgiving we moved in. The summer had been an adventure of watching our house being built. My dad, an amateur photographer, documented the whole process from first shovelful of earth to completion. We were still unpacking and getting used to this new neighborhood when December 7th happened. Under any other circumstances, we would have gradually met our neighbors and settled in, but the war forced faster alliances in the form of volunteer air radio wardens, the paper, metal and grease collectors, children overseen by the parents as they dragged wagons around.

Of course, the three Miller children were enrolled in school as they became of age. I was already in the fifth grade and entered Victory Park School half way through the school year. My sister went to the old Green Road school for her first years. It has since been torn down, but stood about where the KeyBank ATM is now. I wonder if any pictures are still around.

What follows are some random memories from these many years in South Euclid. Libraries were very important to my Mother. Before the library moved to the Telling Mansion it was on the corner of Mayfield Road and Victory Drive. The building is still there. I graduated from Brush High School in 1949. It was seventh through twelfth grade then. As a seventh-grader the seniors seemed very much older. In point of fact many of the males went directly from graduation to the military. My class broke new ground when, for the first time, French was offered in addition to Latin and Spanish. In another daring move three boys made it known that they would rather be enrolled in home economics, which was solely the province of the female students at that time.

This particular semester was cooking and they declared they would rather learn about that. Their only other choice was shop, the male bastion for learning those manly arts such as carpentry, electrical applications and auto repair. To the credit of some forward-thinking people in charge, they were allowed into the cooking class. The teacher, Mrs. King, took it in stride and kept things going even when the boys would draw attention to themselves with what passed for witty repartee as they measured and stirred.

My first job was at Messenger's Restaurant at the corner of Mayfield and Brookline, an easy walk from our home on Plainfield. In the early 1950's in the summer, I was a camp counselor at the day camp held at Rowland School. Again, a short bike ride to work.

During the first years that we lived on Plainfield it was not a through street, but ended at a massive field full of scratchy bushes, a lot of which were blackberry. My grandmother, who lived with us, would take me and my sister with her to pick this fruit which was turned into jam and pies. At least most of it was. We did manage to eat some along the way.

The first Post Office was on Mayfield Road between Plainfield and Winston. It was a sturdy little brick square affair which served the needs before the population began to grow. Mail delivery took place twice a day.

Streetcars ran from downtown, along Euclid Avenue, climbing up Cedar Hill, onto Euclid Heights Boulevard, turning onto Coventry and then onto Mayfield Road. The end of the line was close to the border of South Euclid and Cleveland Heights just half a block from Warrensville Center Road. It backed into an alley-way along side of Wennes Drug Store. That alley is still there, albeit sans tracks. Because of the proximity to this public transit facility, people who lived at the western edge of South Euclid had good access to the city of Cleveland where many worked. Within South Euclid, at least for a while there was the Shephard Bus Company. It ran small buses along Mayfield, probably going no further than Evanston where Brush High is.

The aforementioned Wennes Drug was replaced by Gable Drug store. Mr. and Mrs. Gable were both pharmacists and were our neighbors on Plainfield.

Our dad caused a bit of a stir in the late 1940's when he decided to repaint our white two-story colonial a different color. He had been taken with the red barns he encountered on his trips through rural Ohio. He chose a color called, appropriately, "Barn Red." It's used a lot now but was very daring back in the day. He got a lot of comments, both pro and con, from people passing by.

An annual event called the Ox Roast was held on the grounds of Victory Park School. The school was set back at just about where the

Giant Eagle store is now. The front was grass with a walkway leading up to the school. On that grassy area were stalls selling edibles and such, but the main event was the "Ox" roasting over an open fire on a spit. I suspect it was actually a side of beef, but "Ox" had a certain mystique about it. Workers sliced off pieces of "Ox" and loaded it on buns to be sold to hungry people, probably made hungry by the smell of roasting beef. Inside the school, in the Gym just opposite the main entrance, was a white elephant sale where donated stuff was sold. I think it was either the Kiwanis or Lions club which organized the Ox Roast.

Postwar South Euclid, like so many suburban areas, experienced a growth in population. There was a lot of undeveloped land especially in the area around what is now Bexley Park and Rowland school. Many of the iconic Cape Cods were built and are still there. It's interesting to see how creative people have done interesting things to make these once cookie-cutter homes appear more unique. With all this building came people with children. That's how Rowland School came to be built. Other elementary schools came along, as well as Memorial Junior High and Greenview. In the 1970's and 1980's, with a drop in population, several elementary schools closed.

Some losses occurred as a result of the population growth. One of those which our family would miss were the blackberry fields that were cleared so that Plainfield could be cut through to meet Bluestone Road. On this added piece of road more houses were built.

My husband and I were ready for home ownership and began looking. We found an older home on Ellison Road in 1959. It needed some TLC and we supplied that. All of our children were born there. At the end of Ellison as well, postwar building had taken place, and many children called that street home.

In 1963 my parents moved from the house they had built on Plainfield to Sheridan Road at the east end of South Euclid. They wanted to stay in South Euclid but felt they needed more space. My brother was in junior high and they wanted to stay in the same school system. This is the house that is home to the third and fourth generations of our family now.

After several years away from South Euclid where my parents still lived, we felt we would like to get back into a house, having experienced condo living and found it wanting. A small by-owner ad caught our eye. It seemed to describe exactly the sort of home we were looking for. The only mystery was the street. After so many years in South Euclid I thought I knew the name and location of all the streets, but Belwood did not sound like any that I recognized. Checking the map, there it was, right off Belvoir Boulevard and just a short distance from our first home on Ellison. The street was being developed during the time we lived there. How had I not noticed? We made an offer immediately after seeing it and are enjoying living here going on sixteen years.

Now we are seeing South Euclid, an older inner-ring suburb, adjusting to the twenty-first century. Attention is being paid to older housing stock and environmental issues. All of this is for the best.

I feel that our family has left a legacy in the house that my parents built on Plainfield and continues that legacy through the generations still in residence. Ironically we left a similar legacy in Cleveland Heights by virtue of a house we built there and lived in for twenty eight years. Our family has strong histories in both places.

Centennial

Memories of Childhood around 1950

by Louise Prochaska

Around 1946, the Prochaska family moved to 1200 Avondale, still the gray corner house with the screen porch facing Elmwood. In the first years, there were not too many houses on Avondale going south toward Ardmore, just a few at each corner. The Fire Department came on more than one winter day to build snow banks around 3 empty lots. Then they flooded the area from the fire hydrant, giving us our own skating rink. It was just great! And in summer, my grandmother took me into the fields on these lots where we picked many pints of blackberries.

In early December of 1950, the snow was so deep we didn't have school for a week. We built great snow forts in front of the house. We always walked north on Avondale to St. Margaret Mary School at Belvoir/Bluestone, but after Thanksgiving the snow was 4-5 feet deep. We walked to church on Sunday.

One African-American family moved in on Avondale, a single mom with two children, a girl my age and a little boy. The kids on the street made fun of them, and told their parents false stories that made the parents complain to the mother. A few months later, they moved away. Now I feel guilty for the racism that was so toxic on our mostly Christian street.

Centennial

A Teenager in the 1970s

by Lisa Ann Perry

I grew up in South Euclid and have lived in the South Euclid / Lyndhurst area my entire life. I attended St. John Lutheran School and graduated from Brush High School. Our three children attended Ridgebury Elementary and Greenview Upper Elementary, and graduated from Brush High School. Summers I spent working at Victory Park Pool. I attended Notre Dame College. For years I worked at University Suburban Health Center and other medical facilities in the area. I've been active in the community and its schools and churches. The South Euclid / Lyndhurst area has been my life, but the South Euclid I grew up in is not the South Euclid of today. Change was, and is, inevitable. Change is something we must accept, for if we don't, we are destined to lead a very unhappy life. This is the story of my life, growing up in South Euclid as a teenager in the 1970s.

Mayfield was, and is, the city's main commercial strip. The similarities between past and present stop there. The strip referred to as Maymore Shopping Center, between Marc's and Taco Bell, used to house the BiRite and A&P grocery stores, and between them was a pharmacy. I remember vaguely that the 50th Jubilee of South Euclid was celebrated in the parking lot behind those stores. I was there. I was 8 years old.

Further west on Mayfield, between Marc's and Green Road, I remember a women's dress shop, a men's shop, a pharmacy, a shoe repair shop, a bar and a bank. Across the street were two barber shops (once owned by father and son) and the Swedish bakery, one of the best bakeries ever. Although I was too young to drive, I remember in the early '70s angle-in parking right on Mayfield. I also remember four pharmacies between Maywood Road and Green Road on Mayfield.

Changes were also noticeable on Green Road. The old South Euclid City Hall was torn down to build the new one. Further up Green, I remember when the old Rainbow Hospital, a long-term care facility for handicapped children, was being torn down. Its large front lawn was the end point to many parades that started at Victory Park School. I watched University Suburban Health Center evolve in its place and witnessed the building of its many additions. It later became a primary source of work for me and many of my family members.

These are the memories of my city. This is where I grew up and lived until I got married. After the marriage I lived in South Euclid until the mid '80s when I moved to Lyndhurst. So I have lived in the South Euclid / Lyndhurst area all my life. It has been my life. I wouldn't want it any other way.

Teenage years can be difficult and I know mine were. I attended St. John's elementary school, which was very small, with approximately 200 students total in grades K-8. The education was excellent. We were told to accept all people as God's children but to think a certain way and to fit into a certain mold. Then I moved on to Brush in the heyday of the school system when South Euclid / Lyndhurst schools boasted a total of 9 elementary schools, 2 junior high schools, and Brush. For me, arriving at Brush was a culture shock, to say the least. Here I learned to accept all students with their differences, while remembering we are all equal. My graduating class in 1976 was one of the largest in Brush's history, with approximately 800 students. (In comparison, the class of 2017 had approximately 280 students.)

I remember, on my first visit to Brush, looking up on the hill and noticing how majestic the school looked, and how large it looked, spread out on the hill. Everything was huge. Registering for classes gave me choices, something I had never had before. I could pick classes

I was interested in and get credit for them. I spent years exploring the Metro Parks and Euclid Creek with its many species of plant and animal life. Here at Brush I could not only get credit for this, but I could also meet other students with similar interests and spend time exploring things with them. Amazing.

Even in high school, I always knew I would work in some field of medicine. Happily, I found a group of students who attended monthly labs and lectures in various aspects of medicine at Huron Road Hospital. There were art classes for people who were not necessarily good at basic art techniques but who, like me, wanted to learn different crafts. The one thing that finally put me at ease (or at least helped a lot) was the array of girls' sports. There were teams for every season and I wanted to try them all: swimming, gymnastics, track, cross-country, volleyball and basketball, just to name a few. All this for a student for whom physical education was a close second in terms of her college education. Wow!

Now let's look at school and my experience. I had attended Greenview for a year which helped with my transition from St. John's to Brush, but not much. It took a week or two at Greenview until I felt like I belonged, and realized there were others who felt as lost as I did. Initially I was shy, but with so many people I couldn't help but find someone I could relate to. Sharing classes, exchanging a few words, and getting involved in the many available groups helped me realize that as different as some students seemed, we all shared a common interest within the group. This realization spurred me on to learn more about the nationalities, cultures, and religions of other students. This was something I never thought about, nor was I taught.

Looking back now over 40 years, my three years at Brush High School were among of the high points and greatest memories of my life. As difficult as I thought my teenage years were, they've come to be my favorite memories. Some of the people I met back then are still my friends today.

My joy in swimming led me to enroll in a lifeguard class. My first job was working for the Victory Park Pool staff and I still enjoy teaching swimming today. (Victory Pool was a small neighborhood pool located on Victory Drive in South Euclid, behind what was once Victory Park School, where Giant Eagle is now.) I enjoyed working as a lifeguard, but who wouldn't? The perks of the job included parading around the pool in a bathing suit and getting a good tan! But one has to remember that we were responsible for the lives of swimmers, a great responsibility considering the poor pay we received as part-time summer employees.

Working in a neighborhood had its advantages. The area around the pool in the '70s was mainly Italian families who kept us well fed with pizza and other treats. Next to the pool were the bocce courts, which were never empty. Victory Pool became an area hangout.

After-hours adventures during my teen years included the various carnivals in the area. The yearly Ox Roast and the Lions' Carnival were held in the front yard of Victory Park School. I cannot forget other carnivals in the area, especially those put on by St. Gregory's and St. Margaret Mary's Catholic schools. Of course, for those over 18 (the legal drinking age at the time), there were other popular hangouts, including Carlone's, The Lemon Tree, and our favorite, Gandoff's, with dancing and Sunday night oldies. Sunday nights were great and as we entered our college years, we students looked forward to winter and spring breaks when our other friends came home from college and we all met up at Gandoff's.

South Euclid had so much to offer and still does. As I've said before, change is inevitable, even if it isn't always welcome. The city has accepted the challenge of change and has moved on, all for the positive. For so many years the South Euclid / Lyndhurst area has been my home town. I'm happy here and wouldn't want to be anywhere else.

The is my town. This is my life!

Centennial

Survival on the Playground Slide

by Jay Haarburger

It was January 25th, 1993, and I was a seven-year-old and a first grader at Adrian Elementary School. The day was cold and overcast, with a decent amount of snow on the ground. During recess, the children on the playground decided to put snow on the big orange sliding board to make us go even faster when we slid down. We all took turns going down the slide, and eventually it was my turn. But little did I know at that point that this simple moment of fun would almost turn into the end of my life.

I lay down on my stomach so that I would go down feet first. Of course I was wearing a winter coat, one with plastic beads on it to adjust the strings around the hood. I pushed off and started to go down. But suddenly I stopped, and I couldn't breathe. I was being strangled somehow and was suffocating! At first I thought that someone was intentionally grabbing the string of my hood as a sick joke, and I was getting angry as well as afraid at this sudden and confusing emergency. (A year before, after someone had showed me techniques for efficiently walking up a slide in reverse, I had decided to try it. The combination of anger, fear, and the physical exhaustion of walking back up without respiration resulted in me passing out and losing consciousness.)

The last thing I remembered was looking up at the winter sky with the treetops in the distance, and then, suddenly, nothingness. It was like falling asleep, but with more distress. The physical sensation of being strangled feels first painful and frightening, as I could breathe and, in panic, I tried desperately to inhale, which of course was very painful. But then, I started to focus inward, and the reality around me became distant. I know it was there, but it didn't seem like reality, and sounded distant even with people up close. I started to lose conscious awareness of the world around me and drifted into this blankness and nothingness. Eventually I just blacked out. The next thing I knew I was on the sliding board in a pure black background, and I was going down into infinity, and I was stuck, with the sounds of my classmates' voices screaming far off in the background. I was on a slide and I couldn't get off it and I was permanently stuck to it, or so it seemed. So of course I started panicking and shouting for help.

The next thing I knew, I was waking up in the school infirmary with a paramedic shining a light into my eyes. They explained what happened: As I was going down, one of the beads on my coat got stuck in a hole on the side of the sliding board by pure chance, and as I slid down, the string narrowed around my neck and eventually hanged me on the slide, and I blacked out. While I was unconscious, my classmates were very scared. One of them went to tell the teacher I was being strangled, while another saved my life by pulling the bead out of the hole. It took him eleven tries, and I then slid to the bottom. Luckily, my gym teacher knew CPR and was able to resuscitate me, at which time I started to have the nightmare of being trapped on the slide going down in an infinite spiral.

Adrian's Current Playground Slide

I spent three days in the ICU at the children's hospital in downtown Cleveland, with the doctors fearing that lack of oxygen would cause my brain to swell. Luckily it didn't, and I was released from the hospital three days later. The three people who saved my life were considered heroes. John Spotford was the classmate that went to tell the teachers of the emergency, while Ryan Santa physically pulled the bead out of the slide. The gym teacher, Mrs. Walden, resuscitated me by giving me CPR. All four of us were on the front page of the Plain Dealer the following week, as well in the local Sun Paper. I also had the chance to be on "Rescue 911", but being seven years old, I was overwhelmed by the attention. My incident led to new laws being passed in the manufacturing of children's coats, and it was one of the most significant events of my life.

In 2010, I began work on creating a digital repository of photos of South Euclid-Lyndhurst history, which eventually led to other historical projects and presentations. This project itself rebooted my interest in local history and the revitalization of the historical society. I was also the treasurer of the South Euclid-Lyndhurst Historical Society from 2011 to 2014. I plan on giving more presentations on local historical research in the future. Not only am I grateful for the heroism of my friends and for being here today, but also, through the butterfly effect, this event gradually led me to help preserve and reinvigorate interest in the history of the area. Thus, my friends didn't just save my life, they also helped save the legacy of South Euclid-Lyndhurst as well! (And if you are reading this in the booklet of South Euclid stories, you hold the result of my survival, and my work, in your hands at the moment). This is another great example of the strength and interconnectivity of our home town!

Centennial

The Welos

by Sally Accorti Martin

In 1973, a fifteen-year-old Girl Scout named Georgine Coso competed against Girl Scouts throughout Ohio to participate in "Barriers Down", a national program that allowed Scouts to participate in a service project that would make a difference outside of their community. As Georgine would do so many times in her life, she set her mind to accomplish something, and she did it.

That's how the Willoughby Hills teen who grew up helping her parents farm their land became one of two Ohio scouts selected for the project. She got on a plane for the first time in her life and headed to Tulsa, Oklahoma to work with disadvantaged African-American and Native American preschoolers in an inner-city Head Start program. The experience transformed her life and led to a distinguished career in public service.

Georgine and the other scouts walked the children past the city swimming pool every day as they headed to other outings. "None of the kids' families could afford towels," says Georgine Coso, now South Euclid Mayor Georgine Welo. "That kept them from being able to swim at the public pool, which was how they kept the minority kids out."

The exclusion and underhanded racism continued to bother her. Georgine asked the other scouts to donate their towels to the children, so they could finally have a chance to swim in the pool. That triumphant first swim informed her life choices from that day forward.

Forty-four years later, Georgine Welo is in her fourth term as the Mayor of South Euclid, Ohio. Her rise from Girl Scout, to wife and mother, to distinguished public servant, is a story with many twists and turns.

The oldest of four children of Sam and Dorothy Coso, Georgine lived with her family in Willoughby Hills, where the family farmed part-time to supplement Sam's income as a teacher in Mayfield schools. As first-generation Serbian-Americans, the family's social activities revolved around St. Sava Parish in Parma and the local Serbian community. After achieving First Class Rank in Girl Scouts, Georgine continued her education at the University of Akron, where she pursued a degree in criminal justice and contemplated joining the FBI. In July 1976, Georgine and her high school friends decided to spend an evening at The Palace in Painesville, a choice that would shape the rest of her life. That same night, 21-year-old Carter Welo and his friends decided to make the trek to The Palace in Painesville to celebrate winning a summer bowling tournament. Carter and his friends asked a group of girls from Willoughby South if they could share a table. A pleasant evening of dancing ensued. It would be another six months before Carter and Georgine spoke again, but he never forgot her name. When visiting friends at the University of Akron the following winter, he looked her up in the phone book and arranged a date. By the following autumn they were engaged.

Carter Welo had grown up in a family of nine children in South Euclid on South Green Road, attended St. Gregory the Great School and Cathedral Latin High School. He began working at South Euclid Hardware during high school in 1973. When the owner, Dan Logar, died in 1975, Carter began managing the store and hoped to one day purchase the store. When asked why he has remained a life-long South Euclid resident, Carter explained, "It's like Mayberry. Everyone knows everyone. It's home."

After their 1979 wedding at St. Sava, Georgine decided to leave the University of Akron temporarily to work and help Carter raise enough funds to purchase the hardware store, which they finally did in 1981. The '80s were a busy decade for the Welos as they ran their business, purchased their first home on Victory Drive, and started a family. Daughter Nicky arrived in 1982, followed by sons Carter Jr. in 1984 and Miles in 1988. In 1990, while busy raising her children, Georgine went back to the University of Akron and completed her degree in Political and Environmental Science in 1995.

The Welos quickly became involved in all aspects of community life. Carter was the President of the May-Green Merchants' Association for many years throughout the '80s and into the '90s. He became involved in the St. Gregory the Great Drama Club—first as a set builder, later as an actor—once Georgine let everyone know that Carter just happened to be a great singer. He eventually took over the productions at St. Gregory the Great and reflected on how those plays made a difference in the community.

"We had almost 100 percent participation among the students," Carter said. "Those plays brought all the kids together and brought out the best in them."

His drama career continues today. He has performed in many local productions through the Mercury Theatre Company and in other regional venues.

In addition to their other community activities, Georgine was heavily involved with the South Euclid-Lyndhurst schools. She became active in PTA and various school committees. In 1991, Carter encouraged her to harness her enthusiasm for the community and run for City Council. "She was so passionate about everything she did," Carter says. "When she got involved in something, she jumped in all the way, for all the right reasons."

With his encouragement, she began a grass roots campaign in which her most ardent supporters were other school moms who campaigned by attaching Welo signs to their strollers. She won with the highest vote count ever received by a council candidate in South Euclid. She won the seat for two additional terms, leaving Council in 1998 to accept a position as an Administrative Bailiff in the Court of Common Pleas. City charter at that time required her to resign from Council to accept the position. During her years as a bailiff, she remained involved with the city through service on the city's Planning Commission and myriad volunteer efforts.

In 2002, Georgine was at home doing spring cleaning when a group of residents stopped by to encourage her to run for mayor. Unsure, she attended 26 meet-and-greet events in residents' homes from June through October to determine if she had enough support for her candidacy. On January 3, 2003, she made the decision to run. One of her biggest supporters was her husband Carter, who explained his reasons: "Her cup is always half full," Carter says. "I knew she would be a great mayor and would bring fresh ideas to the city."

Georgine felt that the city had so much untapped potential and that the changes in the city's demographics were exciting and would make the city stronger. And on the 30th anniversary of her competition to win the right to help underprivileged kids in Oklahoma, Georgine competed for the right to help South Euclid residents make their city better, and once again, she won.

On Jan. 1, 2004, Georgine Welo became the first female mayor of the City of South Euclid. She went on to win the seat three more times, in 2007, 2011, and 2015. When reflecting on the biggest challenges and accomplishments she has encountered since becoming mayor, Georgine cites the economic recession and the housing crisis as both the biggest challenge and a crisis turned into an opportunity.

"When I walked the city in 2003, I started to see vacant homes," Georgine says. "I had never seen that in the city before. Because of my work in the courts, I knew this was the tip of the iceberg."

Georgine worked with Judge Richard McMonagle to see how the courts could help, which resulted in the establishment of the County Foreclosure Prevention Program. She convinced the mayors of other inner-ring suburbs to join with her to bring their concerns to the County Commissioners. Georgine saw the need for the region to do more to address vacancy and blight, so she became a key leader in the push to attract attention to the issue.

Realizing that the region had to think differently to manage the crisis, Georgine was one of the initial champions and a founding board member of the Cuyahoga Land Bank. Georgine knew that managing the crisis in South Euclid would take more code enforcement effort than the city had at the time, so she petitioned City Council to establish a new position to oversee the city's housing stock. In 2008, the city's first Housing Manager was hired. Since then the city has taken a leadership role in the management of the housing crisis and has served as a national model for best practices, winning a Crain's Cleveland Emerald Award in 2010 and receiving international press coverage.

Since 2010, the city has seen more than $50 million in residential investment and more than $100 million in commercial development—an impressive accomplishment, given that nearly 30 percent of the city's housing stock has been in foreclosure since the crisis began. For the first time in decades, new homes are being built in neighborhoods throughout the city, bringing new housing options and helping to increase property values.

More than 1000 formerly vacant homes have been renovated and put back into productive use, and home prices continue to rise. One South Euclid, a community development corporation formed in 2009, has assisted in bringing scores of formerly vacant and tax-foreclosed properties back onto the tax rolls. The city has a new brand and a fresh new image that is attracting new homeowners.

From beginning her career in public service as a young mother and continuing it now decades later as a grandmother, Mayor Welo believes that the future is bright for South Euclid. "Generation Y wants a smaller footprint," Georgine says. "They want to shop locally, have access to public transit and be able to take advantage of walkable amenities. We offer all of that. We are no longer just a bedroom community. We are a college town for all ages. I am proud to serve the citizens of South Euclid and be part of our city's renaissance."

South Euclid on the Portage Escarpment: Forces of Landscape Change

by Roy Larick, PhD

South Euclid sits squarely upon the Portage Escarpment, the north-facing slope that joins North America's Central Lowland and Appalachian Highland. On Cleveland's East Side, the escarpment holds Lake Erie against the highland (**Figure 1**). The escarpment also gives rise to our north-flowing watersheds.

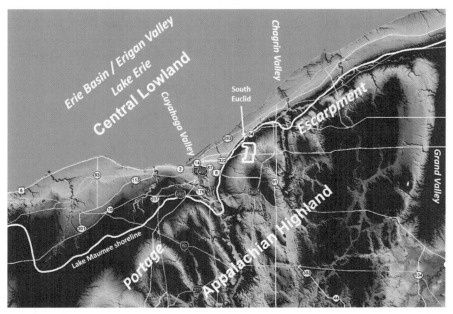

Figure 1 – Regional View

Herein, I outline the forces that have shaped South Euclid's escarpment landscape through the ages. Varied natural events have given a glacially smoothed, north facing shale plateau, punctuated by a couple of hardstone terraces. Upon this landmass, two young streams,

Euclid Creek and Nine Mile Creek, have carved several handsome ravines and one impressive rock-sheltered gulch.

During the last two centuries, humans have forcibly dug in upon this natural landscape, weaving a maze-like built environment of roads, sewers, streets, buildings and parks. Humans are therefore the latest but strongest force of local landscape change. We have not thought much about the consequences of our power over the landscape which has produced several negative consequences. Given shrewd reflection, nevertheless, we now have the chance to reshape the landscape toward ecological diversity and environmental resilience. This is a good task to contemplate during South Euclid's Centennial Year.

A few words about time. There are several "ages" in which strong forces have shaped our place (**Figure 2**). These include the major geological eras or paleontological Life Ages: Paleozoic ("Old Life"), Mesozoic ("Middle Life"), and Cenozoic ("New Life"). Within the Paleozoic Era, I call out the Devonian Period, also known as the Age of Fish.

Era	Period	Epoch	"Age"	Dates
↑	↑	↑	Post-Industrial	1970-present
		Anthropocene		1950-present
			Industrial	1790-1970 CE
		Holocene		12 ka-1950 CE
			Final Glacial	23-12 ka
	Quaternary	Pleistocene	Ice	2.6 Ma-12 ka
Cenozoic			New Life	
Mesozoic			Middle Life	
	Carboniferous			360-300 Ma
Paleozoic	Devonian		Old Life	420-360 Ma

Figure 2 - Ages

It was during the later Devonian, 380-360 Ma (million years ago) that most of our bedrock built up in a shallow sea. In terms of bedrock, we are a Devonian city. Within the present Cenozoic Era, the chronology is more complex. During the Pleistocene (Ice Age), the final glacial advance 23 ka (thousand years ago) led to great landscape change. And then there is the current Anthropocene, which brings human force to a locally post-industrial urban environment.

South Euclid's Portage Escarpment landscape is subtle; it lacks an impressive vertical scale. Yet some local features have special verticality within the East Side Heights, namely the hardstone terrace edges, the shale ravines and the incomparable Euclid Falls gulch. On their own terms, our local landforms shine.

Let's go to the landscape!

Old Life Buildup

About 380 Ma, South Euclid's natural landscape was a seascape, in which we would stand upon a shallow equatorial sea bottom to watch the buildup of sand, silt and clay washed from nearby landmasses. Our position would be near the equator in an area lying, currently, off the Peruvian coast of South America. To the east, the Appalachian Mountains would be rising. South Euclid thus lay in a shallow sea aside a rising mountain

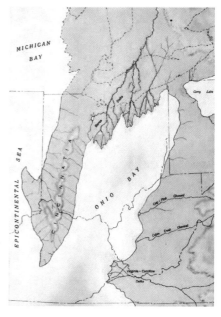

Figure 3 – Ohio Bay

flank configuration called a foreland basin. During the Devonian, we were "Ohio Bay" on the Appalachian west flank (**Figure 3**).[1]

A stack of Devonian sea bottoms can be seen in the Welch Woods cliff, just north of the city (**Figures 4, 5 & 6**). From streambed to plateau top, 120 feet above, the cliff face alternates between thinner/lighter and thicker/darker horizontal beds. The darker layers are shale, representing the buildup of clayey sea bottoms during deeper/calmer conditions; lighter beds are fine sandstone, representing sandy bottoms under shallower/stormier conditions. Most of the cliff face, nearly 80 vertical feet of it, exposes the Chagrin Shale, the oldest Devonian bedrock in our area.

The Age of Fish seas were home to a lot of fish, including two diverse lines of predators: the sharks and the now-extinct arthrodires (placoderms: fish with bony plates covering head and thorax). Normally, we could expect many fish fossils, but the local seas also held many carcass-digesting creatures. Just a few fossils are known: the

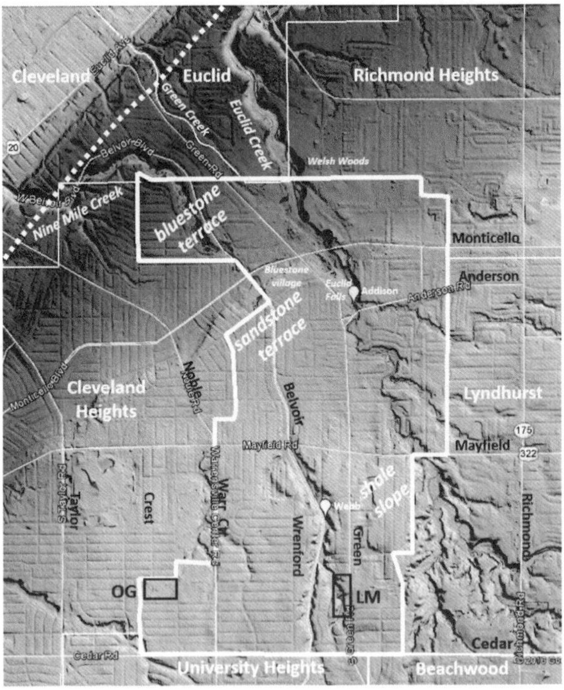

Figure 4 – South Euclid Outline

isolated shark tooth and placoderm plate.

Above the Chagrin, the Cleveland Shale represents a shallower sea yet richer in life. The sea bottoms, about 375 Ma in age, have so much organic material as to appear black in color. The Cleveland has fossils of more than

Figure 5 – Cliff Face at Euclid Creek, Welsh Woods[2]

40 species of fish including very large sharks and arthrodires. The Cleveland is about 30 feet thick in South Euclid and, alas, has very few fossils.

At the very top of the Welsh Woods cliff, the base of the Bedford Shale appears. A more complete exposure can be seen upstream at Cathedral Rock, just below the Monticello Road bridge (**Figures 6, 7 & 8**). Prominent here is the Bedford's most famous local rock unit, the Euclid bluestone.[3] This fine sandstone conserves a patch of sandy sea bottom laid down some 370 Ma. The story is interesting. Near the distant Appalachians, stormy seas churned up the

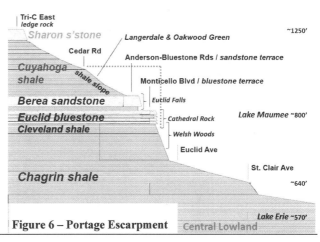

Figure 6 – Portage Escarpment

silty sand which then slid in masses many miles westward to our area.[4] Over time, the masses compressed to become a beautiful fine "bluestone," mostly light gray in color.[5] The seas then quieted and more shale built up on top. In South Euclid, the bluestone beds range up to 30 feet thick.

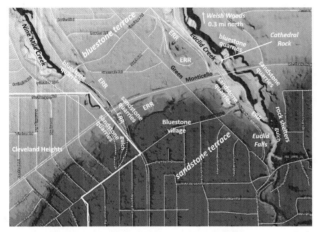

By 365 Ma or so, land had closed in on Ohio Bay. Above the Bedford Shale, the local seascape now held large, south-flowing river channels which carried quartz and other

Figure 7 – Euclid Falls & Bluestone

mineral sands into shallow water (**Figure 3**). (Imagine the current Mississippi River delta encroaching upon the Gulf of Mexico.) As the rivers slowed, their sands built up the bottom, thick in some places and thin in others. During the 1870s, geologists studied massive exposures in Berea and called the whole unit Berea Sandstone. In South

Figure 8 - Cathedral Rock

Euclid, the Berea is 20-30 feet thick and is marvelously exposed in the rock shelters of Euclid Falls (**Figures 6, 7 & 9**).

Figure 9 - Euclid Falls Rock Shelter

Above the Berea, South Euclid's highest rock unit is the Cuyahoga Shale (**Figure 6**), which represents a return to deeper, quieter seas and a steady accumulation of fine silt and clay particles. The Cuyahoga is about 150 feet thick. The southern area of the city, from Cedar to Mayfield Roads, gently descends across the surface of the Cuyahoga Shale, an area I'll call the shale slope (**Figures 4 & 6**). On this shale slope, Nine Mile Creek has cut its Belvoir ravine into the Cuyahoga Shale (**Figure 4**).

With the Cuyahoga Shale, we shift from the Devonian to the Carboniferous Period (**Figure 2**). During the coal age, the Ohio Bay sea bottom accumulated more shale and sandstone and even some limestone and coal. The best known local coal-age rock unit is the Sharon Sandstone, visible as the spectacular plateau-capping ledges at the Chapin Forest Reservation in Kirtland. Closer to home, the Tri-C East campus is built upon Sharon Sandstone ledge rock (**Figure 6**).

Middle Life Uplift/Teardown

After about 200 Ma, eastern North America rose upward out of the sea. Eventually, a broad upland terrace appeared along the western Appalachian foreland. The Ohio Bay sea bottom itself rose many hundreds of feet, enough to bring South Euclid higher than at present.

This rise set the stage for the emergence of our larger north-flowing streams, including the Cuyahoga, Chagrin and Grand (**Figure 1**). These flowed toward a yet larger trunk stream in the Erie basin. This Erigan Valley was the precursor to the Great Lakes watershed from the Upper Lakes eastward to the Saint Lawrence. The Erigan riverbed lay several hundred feet lower than Lake Erie's current bottom. The area's north-facing slope, the formative Portage Escarpment, was substantial. The South Euclid landscape resembled that of Appalachian Southeast Ohio but with greater relief.

In this reversal of fortune—from quiet sea bottom to escarpment highland—much of the rock that had built in the sheltering seas was now torn down and washed away under battering terrestrial rainstorms. Such surface erosion characterized our region for tens of millions of years. During this time, South Euclid lost several rock units that had lain above the Cuyahoga Shale. We can surmise that the city once held a Sharon Sandstone ledge (**Figure 6**).

During the Mesozoic (dinosaur) Era, South Euclid gained its current general topography. The surface of the Cuyahoga Shale achieved the gentle northward descent in the area from Cedar to Mayfield Roads, the area of the shale slope (**Figures 4 & 6**). The much harder Berea Sandstone surface resisted slope cutting and maintained a flat terrace in the area from Mayfield north to Bluestone-Anderson Rds. However, the north edge of the 'sandstone terrace' eroded to form a very steep slope, as seen in the plunge from the Bluestone-Anderson level down to Monticello (**Figures 6 & 7**). Likewise, the resistant surface of the bluestone kept a flat terrace from Monticello northward to the top of Green Hill, where the north edge of the bluestone terrace plunges to Euclid Avenue.

In sum, shallow slopes, flat terraces and steep plunges are the bedrock foundation upon which South Euclid is built.

New Life Ice/Water

Much later, the Northern Hemisphere grew colder and drier. The Ice Age passed from 2.6 Ma to 12 ka, bringing several glacial cycles, each with long/cold and short/warm periods. During the cold, a glacial ice front would advance southward across the Portage Escarpment into central and southwest Ohio. During the warm, the front would retreat northward to expose a fresh landscape. Each advance bulldozed the old bedrock surfaces.

In mountainous terrain, glacial force can cut deep valleys; upon relatively flat landscape, glacial advances tend to shave off summits and dump material into existing valleys. This is the case for our part of the Portage Escarpment where advancing ice fronts ground cap rocks into sand, silt and clay, and then pushed the material into lower areas. Before glaciation, our Appalachian-like summits were higher and more frequent, and valleys were deeper and more numerous. Two and a half million years of glacial action made all slopes gentler.

We know most about the last or final glacial advance which arrived upon the Cleveland area about 23 ka. By this time, the final ice front had pushed southwest, upstream along the Erie basin into western Ohio and Indiana. At Cleveland, the south edge of the glacial front overflowed its Portage Escarpment bank to flow southward into South Euclid and well beyond. Imagine spilled honey moving slowly southward across the 'countertop' of Northeast Ohio. Once again, the final advance planed summits and filled valleys.

Time inevitably brings a reversal of fortune. About 20 ka, the climate warmed and the glacial front began melting back northward. Some 16 ka, the retreating front had reached Shaker Heights. By 14,500 years ago, it lay above Euclid Ave, giving place for our watersheds to be born. Euclid, Nine Mile and Green Creeks formed as rainwater fell upon the bare surfaces left by the retreating ice. The incipient creeks flushed runoff northward toward the retreating glacial front.

As the climate continued to warm, the final ice retreated from the Portage Escarpment and kept moving downstream (northeastward) in the Erie Basin. A series of lakes took the place of the retreating ice of which Lake Erie is, in our eyes, the final product. The first and highest, called Lake Maumee, had its south shoreline at the summits of our local hills: Cedar, Mayfield, Taylor, Chardon, Richmond, etc. (**Figures 1, 4 & 6**). Its north shore lay against the retreating ice, not far northward. Had anyone lived in South Euclid during Lake Maumee's brief stand, they would have had a short walk to the beach—but the water would have been very cold. Water levels fell as the ice retreated and the lakes broadened. Geologists give names to each individual level. Here, we'll say that Lake Erie emerged as 'Canada' became the lake's north shoreline.

About 12.5 ka, Niagara Falls opened and Lake Erie's level descended quickly. Now falling to a lower level, local streams became steeper and carved valleys more quickly. The effect can be seen in the gorges of Euclid and Nine Mile Creeks. Before Niagara, the gorge heads lay not far above Euclid Avenue, near the Lake Maumee shoreline (**Figure 4**). After Niagara, the waterfalls cut their ways upstream nearly two miles in 12,500 years. During this period, Euclid

Creek carved the Welsh Woods and Cathedral Rock cliffs. Currently, the Euclid gorge head lies near Anderson Rd. The Nine Mile Creek gorge head used to extend southward to Bluestone Road; however, as the old quarry areas were filled in to support Belvoir Boulevard, the head has been taken northwest to Princeton Rd (**Figure 7, broken line**).

South Euclid's most impressive erosion feature is historically called Euclid Falls (**Figures 7 & 9**). Here, just north of Anderson Road, Euclid Creek has undercut the Berea Sandstone cliffs to form rock shelters unique on the East Side Heights. Large sandstone blocks have broken off the cliffs to tumble into the creek. Early settlers called this kind of feature a gulch. Farther east in Lake and Geauga Counties, similar features were named Penitentiary Gulch and Stebbins Gulch. Nine Mile Creek probably had a small gulch on the west side of Belvoir between Bluestone and Monticello (**Figure 7**). Quarrying obliterated the rock shelters and the remaining cavity was filled in to support Belvoir Boulevard and Quarry Park.

In sum, the Ice Age transformed an Appalachian-like landscape into a smoothed, low plateau overlying a great, shallow lake. The Portage Escarpment remained the major landform, but much diminished in height and depth from its pre-glacial state. Locally, the prominent remaining features were the sandstone and bluestone terraces, each terminating northward with a low ragged cliff face. Upon this gentle landscape, Euclid, Nine Mile and Green Creeks quickly dug in to make ravines, gorges and gulches. In the increasingly warm post-glacial climate, this fresh landscape acquired ever more temperate forest ecosystems.

Industrial Imprint

In 1796, Moses Cleaveland laid out real estate for the region's industrial rise. Quickly, the Western Reserve's primal forest had to go.

Beyond the need for cropland and firewood, the New England building tradition used hewn timbers for frames and sawn boards for flooring and siding. Euclid Falls provided the best site for water-powered milling. By 1819, William Addison had a sawmill in place at Anderson Road. By 1830, Thomas Webb had one operating on Nine Mile Creek, in the Bayard-Donwell area (**Figure 4**).

Every building and bridge needed a stone foundation; the bedrock terraces provided the material (**Figure 7**). Quarrymen cut foundation stone primarily from the Berea terrace edge on Nine Mile and Euclid Creeks. For the early settlers, bluestone was unnecessarily hard and heavy for use in building. Nevertheless, as cities grew across the eastern U.S., they needed durable sidewalks and wall copings. Bluestone became a favored material. Steam power, for cutting and transporting stone, gave market reach to South Euclid quarries. Bluestone Village (centering on Bluestone Road, between Noble and Green) rose and fell (1870-1915) upon mechanized exploitation of sandstone and bluestone (**Figure 7**).

Regarding landscape, twentieth century manufacturing depended less on local natural resources and more on the need for building platforms. 'Building upon' was the transformative landscape activity. From the 1820s to the 1970s, we steadily remade local landforms into platforms for transport, commerce, and residence. Modern earthmoving technology (steam, then diesel) attacked local landforms much as advancing glaciers had done 23 ka earlier. High points were graded down; ravines were filled in.

Small streams disappeared as their flows were taken into storm sewers and ravines were topped off. Because Euclid Creek was large enough to escape burying, it still runs openly, if narrowly, through the entire city of South Euclid. Smaller Nine Mile Creek was culverted and buried. Nine Mile's South Belvoir ravine remains picturesque but without water. Upper Green Creek holds but a trickle of flow.

In building out the city, we confined nature to a small set of unbuildable locations. Remaining natural landforms are those too difficult to grade down or fill in; the larger features have been incorporated into parks. In 1918, for example, the Cleveland Metropolitan Park System bought the unbuildable Euclid Falls for its Euclid Creek Reservation. On a smaller scale, Quarry Park preserved the Nine Mile Creek gulch area, although totally filled with municipal refuse (**Figure 7**).

Much Industrial Age landscape transformation has been wrought underground. In burying natural streams, we set the stage for very unnatural storm sewer systems or 'sewersheds.' These have been assembled as needed for more than a century. Now, in the face of old age and strong storms, these systems need substantial maintenance and expansion.

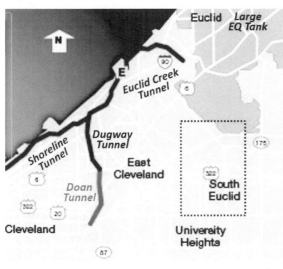

Figure 10 - Storm Sewer Service Areas

The scale of some newer projects is immense. During 2017 the regional sewer district will open the 61 Mg (million gallon) Euclid Creek Storage Tunnel, the first of three such facilities to serve the East Side Heights (Doan and Dugway tunnels come next) (**Figure 10**). Also in

2017, the Euclid Sewer District will open its Large Equalization Tank (15 Mg) to serve South Euclid's northeast corner. While lying outside our borders, these major landscape features respond directly to South Euclid's stormwater needs. And they constitute the strongest landscape-shaping forces seen locally since the final glacial advance.

Massive underground storage represents the "gray" approach to managing stormwater. Under gray, storm runoff is a waste to be cleansed before being delivered to Lake Erie. To solve the stormwater "problem," we build great sewersheds to increase the capacity of over-used natural watersheds.

Anthropocene: Green Reset?

The Anthropocene (**Figure 2**) is the current age in which humans significantly influence earth's climate and ecosystems. The human effect is great enough to be seen in new rocks formed around the globe. They carry uniquely human signatures such as atomic bomb debris. For the South Euclid landscape, the Anthropocene brings a new set of human-influenced forces of change.

The Portage Escarpment lies in the relatively cool, humid part of North America where our urban landscape is generally wet. Now, the area is apparently getting wetter, with more rainfall and storm runoff expected as the new norm. Yet as more water now enters our urban systems, the cost of eliminating moisture increases.

At the same time, new economic forces shape South Euclid. During the last half century, regional manufacturing has contracted and attendant economic sectors have slowed. In relation to its post-WW2 heyday, South Euclid is now a mature city with a built environment somewhat large for its current population. "Urban shrinkage" describes the situation. Shrinkage is lamented as negative growth; nevertheless, with diminished development pressure, the urban landscape takes on new qualities. As built environments retreat, remnant landforms and ecologies tend to reappear. Lost natural legacy comes to light.

Working in tandem, re-emergent green spaces and wet ecosystems can be urban resources. With them, we may move beyond the mindset of landscape platforms and sewersheds. There are two guiding principles: Keep runoff in place, and use it to build local ecological diversity in urban wetlands.

With "green" infrastructure, rainfall runoff is held at or near its point of impact upon the landscape. Instead of massive, centralized sewersheds, we can have many small, distributed storage facilities. Under the concept of bioretention, specialized plant and soil combinations can sequester and ground-infiltrate rainfall in place. With runoff kept out of the sewer system, the need for gray facilities is diminished. In the Anthropocene, distributed green infrastructure is an important complement to centralized gray systems.

Wetlands are most productive ecological features, very efficient at absorbing sunlight to feed the food chain. Wetlands have, per acre, the greatest natural ability to produce life and process wastes. Nearly all great cities have grown upon wetlands, including Cleveland. While nearly all cities have destroyed these environments, many are regenerating critical features and functions. Bioretention is the key urban feature.

Figure 11 - Langerdale Marsh

Currently, South Euclid has two large bioretention-assisted wetlands, both in the shale slope area of Nine Mile Creek (**Figures 4 & 6**). Langerdale Marsh (10 acres) was conceived by City of South Euclid with the Euclid Creek Council and the Cuyahoga Soil and Water Conservation District, and designed by Biohabitats (**Figure 11**). Oakwood Green (5.5 acres) was developed by First Interstate Properties with the City of South Euclid, and designed by Neff & Associates (**Figure 12**).

Langerdale Marsh and Oakwood Green are very important urban wetland projects on the East Side Heights. They make good use of the shale slope landscape, and enhance natural life where we need it most. Future action can forge ecological links

Figure 12 - Oakwood Green Wetlands

between these wetlands and other significant stream-course green spaces such as Euclid Falls and Quarry Park. Linked wetlands are the means to regenerate ecological function across the city.

All such water features tie into one or more of South Euclid's ever-wetter watersheds: Euclid Creek, Nine Mile Creek and Green Creek. In addition to regenerated wetlands, smaller-scale means to rebuild watershed integrity are coming to light. Under Ohio EPA guidance, stream impairments are now better quantified and impairment sources are better identified. Watershed health can now focus upon the most significant current issue: non-point source pollution—runoff that picks up landscape pollutants and carries them to streams. During 2017, non-point source action plans will be assembled for the three South Euclid watersheds,[6] including studies of erosion within the city's small ravines now exacerbated by climate change.

In sum, South Euclid is beginning to see landscape as more than platforms for narrowly-defined economic development. Our watersheds give life to the city and perform valuable ecological services. With stormwater as a resource, it can be managed in place to save money, to create habitat, and to improve local well-being. Bioretention-assisted wetlands give nature a foothold within the city. Linked wetlands enhance eco-diversity across the city. In a green reset, small-scale landforms are primary re-emergent natural capital. In treating these natural features wisely, humans can become a more positive force in shaping place.

Past to Future

South Euclid's bedrocks were built up and torn down in the truly ancient past. Our place rose upon a patch of blue-sand sea bottom laid down 370 million years ago. Much more recently, glacial ice smoothed the rocky landscape. And during yet more recent millennia, Euclid and Nine Mile Creeks have drilled through bluestone and shale to give us handsome ravines within a gently rolling plateau.

In a place-defining moment, Moses Cleaveland staked out the region's industrial real estate. As creeks powered mills and exposed the sandstones for market, South Euclid rose out of the primal forest. New modes of transportation helped build the village and city. Electrified rails brought summer resorts and country estates; automobiles ferried suburbanites to Tudor side streets. And, eventually, interstate highways beckoned residents eastward to newer shopping centers and larger homes.

We now face yet another inflection point. With increased rainfall, it is time to rethink sewersheds. With urban shrinkage, it is time to rethink greenspace. The East Side Portage Escarpment now reverts some toward nature and regenerates ecological function. Watersheds are the new growth landscapes; wetlands are the productive units. Using bioretention, we can manage stormwater, sequester carbon and clean air.

South Euclid can take stock of its natural legacy and of the two centuries in which we transformed nature, not always for her—or our—long-term benefit. In this Centennial Year, let's get out on the landscape to celebrate what we have and to contemplate its future. Let's plan to enhance isolated green spaces and restore natural channels of ecological flow. We can achieve a place that values its natural roots and plans for their sustainable future.

Cf. Notes Section for endnotes and full figure captions.

Our First Visitors: American Indians

by Rebecca Jones Macko

We aren't the first people to walk the shores of Lake Erie. Thousands of years before Europeans arrived in the Western Hemisphere, other peoples were living throughout North America, including here in Northeast Ohio. During the thousands of years of human occupation, peoples prospered, struggled, endured. These people left a legacy written on the landscape that reminds us that we follow in a long line of human occupation.

The first American Indian peoples may have arrived here as early as 11,500 years ago, following large game like mastodon and giant elk. Today archaeologists call these people paleo-Indians. These nomadic bands left very little behind, perhaps an occasional spear point or scar from a fire.

About 10,000 years ago, human culture began to change as the Ice Age ended. The mastodon and giant elk were gone, but people continued hunting and gathering. Still nomadic, these peoples weren't tied to following large game, but moved wherever the hunting, fishing, or gathering was rich at the moment. Archaeologists find more unique artwork, like gorgets, and more artifacts like stone axes.

Two thousand years before Columbus landed in the "New" World, culture changed again. Archaeologists call this new culture the Woodland culture. This culture is like no other culture before it, and it left a legacy written on the land in earthworks. These Woodland peoples begin the first domestication of plants, cultivating sunflowers, *Chenopodium*, Marshelder, Maygrass, Little Barley and Knotweed. The domestication of plants meant a less nomadic lifestyle, as the people settled in some areas for longer periods of time. With the domestication of plants, the never-ending need to find food abates a bit. With the people's newly discovered spare time, their rich artistic culture flourished, leaving carved pipes, pottery, points and bladelets.

One of these Woodland groups was called the Adena peoples. They created giant effigy-like earthworks, the best known being the Serpent Mound in southern Ohio. This culture, and its near cousin, the Hopewell culture, fostered a trade network. The Hopewell stretched that network to upper Michigan, to the North Carolina shores, to Florida, and west to the area today known as Yellowstone. The Hopewell peoples traded for copper, mica, shells and obsidian, bringing them back to Ohio and shaping them into masks, chest pieces, beads, great effigy forms, and surgically-sharp bladelets. Throughout the Cuyahoga Valley we find evidence of the Hopewell peoples in the fire pits, points, and bladelets they left behind. At one time, Hopewellian mounds dotted the valley landscape, but sadly, most have been plowed down or destroyed. A question remains though: why would a culture travel for hundreds of miles to trade for exotic items? What were they trading in turn? And why build mounds?

In time, the people's culture changed again and in the Late Woodland period, about 1000 years ago, American Indian peoples spread the domestication of the familiar agricultural commodities of corn, beans and squash. These "three sisters" require a settled lifestyle and protection from animals, both four-legged and two-legged. They used the latest technological advancement in warfare: the bow and arrow. We also see various groups settling into walled village sites. Remnants of one of those village sites once existed along the wall of the Cuyahoga Valley in an area known as South Park. These sites were studied extensively in the nineteenth century by Charles Whittlesey; the culture in northeast Ohio became known as the Whittlesey Culture.

As the Late Woodland culture flourished about 600 years ago, a new culture arrived on the eastern shore of North America. As Europeans landed, so did their diseases. Trading networks were still in place, and even if interior American Indians had never seen a European, they traded with people who had traded with people who had. And disease spread. Some historians think a third of the American Indian population may have been wiped out by diseases to which the natives had no immunity, like the plague, whooping cough, and different strains of influenza. Others place the numbers lower.

Prior to contact, here in Ohio, American Indians were living in large village sites along river banks and farming on a large scale. Large tracts of land were kept open for agriculture, even as other areas of the land were moved and shaped into earthworks. Now imagine a third of the people in your town/village getting wiped out by a disease you have never experienced before. Who becomes mayor/chief? Who leads you when the elders are all gone? Who keeps your stories, your culture, alive?

For a time, Ohio was less populated. Fields that had once been kept open for corn, beans and squash returned to deep bottomland forest, or, as in the Picqua plains, became grasslands. When Europeans explored Lake Erie, starting with Louis Joliet in the late 17th century, they found a densely forested, sparsely inhabited Ohio country. As trade and competition between the French and English accelerated, various groups of Erie, Lenape (Delaware), Mingo, Iroquois, and others migrated in and out of northern Ohio, most never staying long. At least, archaeologists have not found remains of large, long-inhabited village sites. American Indians found themselves pulled this way and that way in the competition and drive for power in the fur trade. A group might align itself with the English, while the tribe might align with the French. With each war and détente, new alliances were formed and broken. In the late 18th century, yet another nation entered the fray, with the American colonies gaining their freedom. The power struggles became three-way.

We find written references to various trading posts, the earliest being French, one near today's Merriman Valley, another near the mouth of the Cuyahoga. Lorenzo Carter paid $47.50 for two acres of land on the western bank of the Cuyahoga River 220 years ago, and settled in the newly surveyed city of Cleaveland as its first settler. He made friends with the American Indians who travelled nearby, including one Chief Seneca (Stigwanish). This friendship with American Indians would keep the struggling settlement going during its first few years, as the people fought disease, floods and poor crops.

We know the rest of the story. The doors to the Ohio country had been opened and settlers flooded in. There were conflicts, setbacks, peaceful exchanges and scares. At one point, the American Indian alliances very nearly stopped westward expansion, as Tecumseh gathered nations to the west during the War of 1812. But it was only a lull in the relentless march west. Finally, in 1843, the last group of Wendats (Wyandote) were shipped west to reservations by canal boat.

That doesn't mean American Indians are no longer in Ohio. Some chose to give up tribal identity and remained. In the 20th century, with jobs booming in Cleveland, some Indians returned. No longer the numbers they once were, American Indians who remain take pride in their heritage. And they look to the land: it remembers the bustling walled villages, the power struggles of little trading posts, the thousands of baskets of dirt hauled to create one mound, the food and flint remains of some Hopewell Indians' dinner 2000 years ago.

Cf. References Section for list of sources.

Centennial

South Euclid in the Western Reserve:
The Legacy of Euclid Township

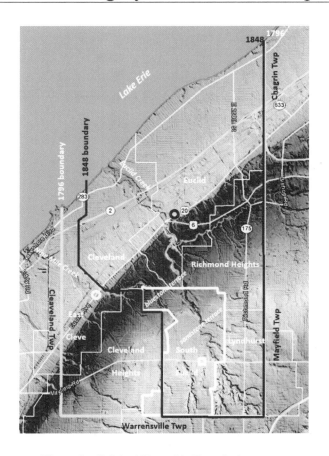

Figure 1 – Original Township Boundaries

South Euclid descends from a 1796 land contract negotiated between Moses Cleaveland and 41 disgruntled members of his Connecticut Land Company survey crew. The contract specified boundaries and owner responsibilities for New Connecticut's largest township. The new owners called the place Euclid, to honor the Greek inventor of surveying geometry (**Figure 1**). Cleaveland and the surveyors signed the transfer on September 30, 1796. During the next 130 years, numerous political secessions broke the township into small municipalities. Among the descendants, the cities of Euclid and South Euclid retain the township's 1796 name.

Founding Documents

In December 1795, the Connecticut Land Company hired Moses Cleaveland to lay out the boundaries and townships of the Connecticut Western Reserve. On July 4, 1796, Superintendent Cleaveland and a crew of 50 men and women arrived at Conneaut to begin work. Several teams set out to define the Township and Range grid lines. Throughout the summer, most of the surveyors suffered from chronic hunger, malaria and dysentery. With the township work complete in late September, the teams assembled at the mouth of the Cuyahoga River. The rank-and-file made their hardships known to Cleaveland. At this meeting, 41 protestors threatened a breach of contract, that is, to not return to complete the survey during its second scheduled year in 1797.[1]

In the meantime, the crew officers had mapped all 128 surveyed townships and ranked them in terms of natural resources and transportation channels. Among the ten best was T8 R11, located immediately east of the capital township **(Figure 1)**. In return for their continued loyalty—for agreeing to return in 1797—Cleaveland offered the protestors the chance to buy and settle T8 R11 in its entirety. In his personal diary, Cleaveland mentioned the evolving T8 R11 negotiations during the last two weeks of September 1796.[2]

A contract for the purchase and settlement of the township was defined in three documents dated September 30, 1796, all of which have survived and are archived at the Western Reserve Historical Society. One is the T8 R11 title agreement signed by Cleaveland and the protestors.[3] A second records the protestors' own meeting to organize their settlement schedule.[4] Third is the land division scheme and the results of a lottery for distributing four lots to each of the 41 signers.[5] An additional surviving document is protestor Moses Warren's field notes which, on September 30, recorded the name 'Euclid' for T8 R11.[6]

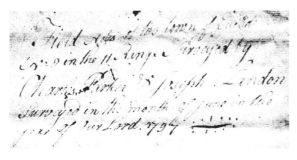

Figure 2 - Surveyor Field Notes

Two weeks later, the survey crew left the Cuyahoga settlement, sailing eastward on Lake Erie for home. On Oct 16, as they passed the mouth of their township's largest stream, the owning surveyors named it Euclid Creek.[7] (The name of South Euclid's second stream, "Nine Mile Creek," is of unsubstantiated origin.[8])

The following summer, June 1797, a protestor team ran 250 miles of survey lines to define the 164 Euclid Contract lots (**Figure 2**).[9] Some of the cleared

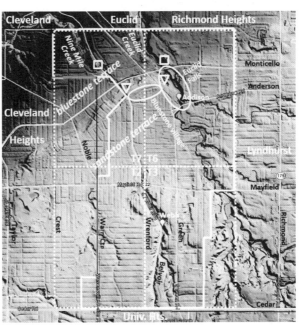

Figure 3 - Topology & Tracts

lines were soon appropriated for roads, streets and major real estate boundaries. The contract did not last, however, as very few of the owners actually came back to the Reserve to fulfill their obligations. The settlement endeavor was dissolved in 1800, and during the summer of 1801, the Connecticut Land Company had the unsold land resurveyed into thousand-acre tracts.[10] South Euclid came to encompass most of Tracts 2, 3, 6 and 7 (**Figure 3**). Within these tracts, the Cuyahoga County Recorder still uses the Original Lot numbers of 1796 to define real property within the city.

Administrative Linkages

In 1796, the Connecticut Western Reserve was laid out within the Northwest Territory as established in 1786, with its capital at Marietta. Within the Territory, much of what later became eastern Ohio lay within a very large Washington County. In 1800 Connecticut's Western Reserve became the County of Trumbull, carved out of Washington County and named after the current Connecticut governor. When Ohio achieved statehood in 1803, the Ohio General Assembly began administrating county charters. In 1805 the assembly moved to break up Trumbull County. The first act was to create Geauga County, which incorporated on March 1, 1806. Cuyahoga County was separated from Geauga in the latter months of 1810.

Township Charter

On March 14, 1810, the Geauga County Commissioners wrote an entitlement to the residents of Euclid to elect township officers on the first Monday of April, 1810 (**Figure 4**).[11]

Figure 4 - Euclid Township Charter

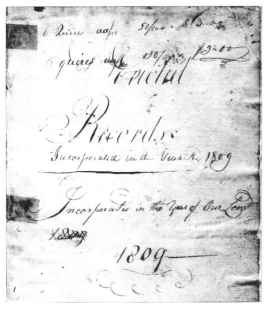

Figure 5 - *Euclid Records* frontispiece

On April 2, the newly elected Euclid Township Trustees recorded their election in a public document, thus beginning the *Euclid Records*, which, over the next 110 years, grew to four large volumes.[12] The *Records'* frontispiece refers to the township's administrative incorporation in 1809 (**Figure 5**). However, the oldest known primary chartering document is the Geauga Commissioners' order, which preceded the administrative function of Cuyahoga County later in the year.

Early Township Life

By 1805, a few families had settled in two places along the Buffalo Road (present-day Euclid Avenue), each near the place where a sizeable stream flowing from its Portage Escarpment gorge crossed the road (**Figure 1**). The hamlets took the name of their streams: Nine Mile Creek and Euclid Creek, respectively. Population grew more rapidly near the gorge mouths than on the Portage Escarpment uplands. but natural resources eventually drew a few families to the area later called South Euclid, where sawmilling and stone quarrying were the earliest activities.

The Euclid survey of 1797 identified Euclid Falls (Anderson Road east of Green) as a possible area for water-powered industry (**Figure 3**). By 1819, William Addison had erected a sawmill there (**Figure 6**). By 1830, Thomas D. Webb built a sawmill on upper Nine Mile Creek; the mill pond and race were in the Bayard-Donwell Drive area just east of the creek.

Every building and bridge needed a stone foundation. High quality building stone was exposed in the terraced landscape in the northern parts of Tracts 6 and 7. In this area, Euclid and Nine Mile Creeks cut through the sandstone and bluestone terraces, giving

Valuable Property
FOR SALE.

THE subscriber offers for sale, all or part (as may suit the purchaser) of Lot No. 26, in Tract No. 6, at the Euclid Falls, on the most reasonable terms for cash. There is on the premises a good saw-mill in operation, and a convenient dwelling house.—For further particulars, enquire of the subscriber at the Falls.

WM. ADDISON, Jr.
Euclid, Dec. 20, 1819.   10—3

Figure 6 - *Cleveland Herald* ad

easy access for quarrying (**Figure 3**).[13] Josephus Hendershott and Isaac Husong began quarrying here during the 1820s. Commercial quarrying developed in the 1870s, with steam used to cut stone and transport it by rail. Bluestone Village (centering on Bluestone Road between Noble and Green) rose and fell (1870-1915) on commercial quarrying of sandstone and bluestone (**Figure 3**).

By the late 1810s, as daily east-west movements through the southern part of the township made use of informal trails, it became clear that a road was needed. In 1828, the State of Ohio provided funds for a State Road, a 60-foot wide cleared path along the old routes (**Figure 3**).[14] The names in current use, Mayfield and US 322, would come later. The State Road represented the first infrastructure improvement made by anything but the labor of township residents. It is at this point that the intersection of Green and Mayfield began to draw permanent settlers. South Euclid had a focal point.

During the mid-1820s, several hamlets gained enough families to warrant separate school districts. In 1828, the *Euclid Records* noted 10 districts, with Number 5 serving the core South Euclid families of the day.[15]

Township Fragmentation

By the 1840s, manufacturing and European immigration were changing the face of Cleveland. The founding New England lifeways and allegiance to a political Western Reserve, and Euclid Township, waned. In 1847, the Nine Mile Creek community formally separated from Euclid to form East Cleveland Township **(Figure 1)**, and the village became known as Collamer. At this point, Euclid Township's administration was focused at Euclid Creek where a town hall was built in 1851. In 1852, the Lake Erie and Ashtabula (now CSX) Railroad was completed through the township, giving Euclid freight and passenger stations on the line. Large-market agriculture and, increasingly, manufacturing drove the local economy.

Around the township, several hamlets acquired enough residents to be granted a U.S. Post Office, a process which formalized names for South Euclid (Mayfield at Green), Euclidville (Mayfield at Richmond) and Claribel (Richmond at Highland), among others.

By the late 1890s, the largest of the hamlets had 1600 residents, enough to be chartered as independent villages within the State of Ohio. Among the first wave were the villages of East Cleveland (1896), Collinwood (1898) and Nottingham (1899). A second wave came during the first years of the twentieth century with Euclid (1903) and Cleveland Heights (1905). Euclid Village retained the town hall at Euclid Creek and all township governmental records. The last chapter of the township's dissolution came during the booming 1910s, as the smallest of the hamlets gained 1600 residents. Chartered in this wave, all in 1917, were South Euclid, Claribel (later renamed Richmond Heights) and Euclidville (soon to be called Lyndhurst). The City of Cleveland annexed Collinwood and Nottingham Villages in 1910 and 1911, respectively. All surviving villages later reincorporated as cities.

Conclusion

South Euclid residents sometimes lament the nature of the city name: south of an old manufacturing center now struggling in a post-industrial era. Yet we must remember that Euclid, the township, was a distinctive manifestation of struggle in the untamed Connecticut Western Reserve. In September 1796, Moses Cleaveland offered the township as recompense for his crew's ordeals with chronic hunger, mosquito fever and dysentery. The 41 protestors committed themselves to build a model settlement in this place. In its name, then, South Euclid recalls an eighteenth-century egalitarianism and idealism that can still stir us two centuries later. And the survey lines of 1797 are yet evident as roads, streets and real estate boundaries. Life in South Euclid thus follows lines laid down by veterans and immediate sons and daughters of the Revolutionary War. The egalitarian settlement did not endure, but its compass bearings and chain readings continue to shape life on the terraces and creeks of South Euclid.

Cf. Notes Section for endnotes and full figure captions.

Euclid Creek Reservation and the Civilian Conservation Corps

by Laura Peskin

The author acknowledges Judy MacKeigan, Foster Brown and Deb Marcinski of Cleveland Metroparks for their indispensable help

Almost as long as South Euclid has been a village, it has shared the 100-year-old Euclid Creek Reservation with the city of Euclid. This year of 2017, as South Euclid celebrates its centennial, both Cleveland Metroparks (originally the Cleveland Metropolitan Park District) and Euclid Creek Reservation celebrate theirs.

One initial goal in building a park system was preserving the area's scenic river valleys. In the especially isolated and scenic Euclid Creek valley, a YMCA cabin near Highland Road and its surroundings constituted the original Euclid Creek Reservation. In 1918 property owners along the eastern branch of Euclid Creek, south of Euclid Avenue and east to the juncture of Chardon and Richmond Roads in Claribel (later Richmond Heights), were amenable to a Metropark land survey and the possibility of donating their land for a park. Yet a park along the east branch of Euclid Creek was

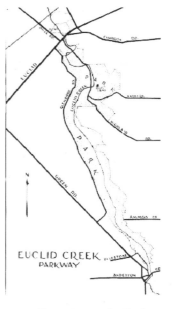

complicated by the fact that some land further northeast was in Lake County, not Cuyahoga. The southern branch of Euclid Creek proved more auspicious for a park, particularly south of Euclid Avenue. The park district quickly saw the impracticality of building a park north of Euclid Avenue, where industry had so transformed the land that it would be difficult to naturalize it into park space. While both Wildwood Marina and Villa Angela Beach on the mouth of Euclid Creek have been public parks since 1933 and the mid-1990s respectively, they only became part of Cleveland Metroparks in 2013.

In its 1919 *Annual Report*, the park board acknowledged that voluntary land donations directly south of Euclid Avenue were proceeding sluggishly, and that the park planned to buy 50 acres at Euclid Avenue and Highland Road, a purchase that was soon executed, making the area accessible to the public. With the buy, Euclid Creek Reservation expanded at the same rate as the new Hinckley and Brecksville Reservations, in southern Cuyahoga County. The Cleveland Metroparks' initial reservation, Rocky River on the West Side of Cleveland, was growing rapidly; Big Creek Park, another pre-1920s West Side park, was showing modest growth in the 1920s. Meanwhile, Bedford Reservation in the Tinkers Creek valley, as well as North Chagrin, South Chagrin and Mill Stream Reservations were getting underway. A key factor which enabled the entire "emerald necklace" of parks ringing Cleveland, a vision since 1905, to become reality was a 1915 change in state law allowing the park district to receive public revenue.

Some reservations became park-like faster than others; Euclid Creek Reservation took some time. In the autumn of the Stock Market crash (1929), the park's only amenities were at Highland Road, although the park already stretched north of Bluestone Road into South Euclid. Still, the park's picnic areas were the second most used after those in Rocky River Reservation (not counting Huntington Beach). The 1930 *Annual Report* asserted that completing the Euclid Creek Reservation was the park district's top priority. Indeed the park was shaping up just when throngs of newly-unemployed people and their families were going to the parks in droves for reasons of serenity in tough times, as well as to simply take advantage of their new-found, if involuntary, leisure time. The 1930 *Annual Report* noted progress at Euclid Creek included considerable clearing of brush and expanded picnic facilities. The park had also developed ball fields, connected to city water, and dammed Euclid Creek to create a swimming pool. (The dam was removed in 2010 in the interest of spawning fish.) The *Report* praised the diverse habitat and terrain at Euclid Creek. While the high southern section of the park was largely former quarries, the northern bottomlands boasted unusual tree species such as Chestnut Oak and Paw-paw.

In 1931 Euclid Creek Park acquired the Luster house site in South Euclid, across the creek from the later Quarry Picnic Area; under negotiation were the neighboring Nellie Wood, Board of Education and other properties. (See the 1930 park map accompanying this essay.) However, no new amenities had been added, prompting the 1931 *Annual Report* to call the park "primitive." The report marveled how close to the factories north of Euclid Avenue was the contrasting forested lower section of the park. The report pointed out the easy access by streetcar to this wilderness, important in that era of high demand for parks by those of limited means.

A sign of the desperate times was the 1932 park district decision to allow the unemployed to remove dead or storm-felled trees for fuel. A new playground at Euclid Creek added cheer. Yet in the Great Depression years before President Franklin Roosevelt was elected, the park district had been foundering financially with land purchases frozen. All available money was being used for park improvement, including hiring additional workers from among those sidelined by the sour economy. Finally help came from the Roosevelt administration's response to the Depression. First, federal grants and loans furnished the park district $650,000 which allowed for the grading of Euclid Creek parkway from Highland Road south to Anderson Road, and the construction of a shelter house, as well as similar improvements in other Metroparks. From grants or other funds, Euclid Creek's parking areas were ameliorated and other upgrades were made.

Another boost to the Metroparks was the organization of armies of previously unemployed, hired by Roosevelt's New Deal agencies, who appeared on the scene to provide inexpensive labor for park improvement. One such agency, the Civilian Conservation Corps (CCC), was a cooperative effort among the Department of the Interior, the War Department, and other branches of government that in its nationwide, eight-year lifespan recruited 300,000 males as young as 17 who were willing to remit most of their earnings to their families.

The CCC's official purpose was to shape the nation's natural resources, land and water. CCC enrollees planted tens of millions of seedlings, built dams, reclaimed soil and the like. Many enrollees shipped to Western states got to experience their immense natural beauty. A good number of the CCC enrollees did the same sort of work in their home states. By 1936 the CCC, the Works Progress Administration (WPA), and related agencies had supplied 5000 men, many from Northeast Ohio, to spruce up the fledgling Cleveland Metroparks. Along with private contractors, they cleared and graded parking and picnic areas, planted and transplanted greenery, and built roads, trails, retaining walls, shelters and more. The creation of all these amenities was especially welcome in Euclid Creek Reservation, a particularly unruly park from the standpoints of recreation, soil conservation/erosion control, and habitat for a variety of native wildlife.

The CCC was one product of Roosevelt's first hundred days in office that brought lasting change to the nation, as was the Federal Deposit Insurance Corporation (FDIC). There were 51 CCC camps in Ohio by 1937, very few near cities. By this same time, 75,000 Ohioans had served in the CCC, a little over half within Ohio.

Being unemployed was a requirement to join the CCC. In fact, both the official literature and surveys of participants show that, more than furthering either the education or the job skills of participants—a claim also made but without much rigorous data in today's terms to back it up with regard to the Ohio CCC men—the overarching CCC goal was to provide income to destitute families and strengthen the businesses contracting with the CCC or patronized by local CCC camp men. While CCC enrollees gave mixed reviews to the leadership, assignments, provisions, quality of instruction and on-the-job training, they and organizers agreed that the CCC, in addition to paying an allowance, improved participants' health and nutritional status, while also lifting attitude and morale. National CCC director Robert Fechner indicated as much himself; Lester Gallogly, in his 1936 university study on the Ohio CCC, found that from the many optional academic, vocational and other classes offered in CCC camps, enrollees gravitated to course work on health or safety, or motivational talks or religious services. At best, the CCC was a substitute for college for its young men; Ohio CCC enrollees on average had a ninth-grade education. Learning how to get along in the world was of utmost importance. John Mizik, a local CCC camp athlete and associate camp newspaper editor, wrote at the time of his spring 1936 discharge: "My most valuable experience as leader was meeting so many degrees of temperaments and abilities and being able to cope with situations arising from such a mixture."

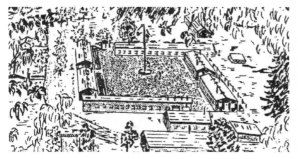

Lange's 1935 drawing of CCC camp

Conveniently, an area CCC base camp, Camp Euclid was located in Euclid Creek Reservation from 1933-1941. The camp was south of Highland Road and south of the then-unfinished parkway up to Anderson Road. (That parkway was later replaced by the present one, about 500 yards to the north.) The camp opened in December 1933 at full capacity of 200 men. (All CCC camps had space for 200.) Additionally, Ohio CCC enrollees who would be stationed out-of-state underwent orientation at Camp Euclid.

In 1934, within six weeks of Camp Euclid's establishment, CCC resident enrollees had blazed an eight-foot wide trail up the gorge as far as Welsh Woods. Here on the South Euclid border, on existing stone abutments, the CCC constructed a 12' x 20' foot bridge across the creek, in order for parkgoers to appreciate up-close the 400+ million years old Cleveland and Chagrin shales on the exposed cliff face. Welsh Woods was leveled for parkgoer use by blasting out solid rock.

CCC wall remnant in Welsh Woods

This difficult undertaking was testament to South Euclid's rich quarrying history. While bluestone had been quarried in Cuyahoga County since the early 1800s, some of the nation's largest quarries developed along Euclid Creek after the Civil War. The earliest was Duncan McFarland's large one; other important nearby quarries in the late 19th century were Forest City Stone, Maxwell & Malone, and Slawson Meeker. In the 1890s, the village of Bluestone, Ohio—analogous to a Western boomtown with tar paper worker shacks, a post office, saloons, and a temperance hall—sprang up near Anderson and Green Roads. Its Swedish Evangelical Lutheran church, erected for immigrant workers on Malone Quarry land, was torn down in 1930 when the Metroparks purchased its land at the northwest corner of East Green and Anderson Roads. By the 1940s, the main remnant of the area bluestone industry was still operational as South Euclid Stone and Supply quarry. Alas, cement had displaced bluestone for its most desired use, sidewalk slabs, even though stone ones are more attractive and durable.

The plentiful supply of bluestone from the quarry lands provided building material that was worked expertly by the CCC or WPA laborers on many projects including stone retaining walls. It was general CCC procedure to use local materials that would harmonize with surroundings. Newton Bishop Drury (National Park Service director 1940-1951) further remarked, "Some of the most attractive masonry [in parks] had been furnished in the CCC days when these boys who went into the camps had a flair for stone work." Erosion has all but obliterated some of this fine stonework, including the wall above Euclid Creek at the Welsh Woods geological site. (See 1936 CCC stonework photo and 1940 and 2017 Welsh Woods shale photos accompanying this essay.) Yet one can still admire CCC masonry in the park today.

Planting an ill-fated American Elm

By 1937, with all the CCC hours logged, Euclid Creek Reservation had over four miles of trails and bridle paths, nearly a dozen improved picnic areas, three playing fields, eight bridges and more. The CCC made the reservation's former South Euclid stone quarries look like a sylvan retreat. In 1936 and 1937 alone, the CCC planted almost 2000 native trees, including Black Locust, White Pine, Eastern Redbud, Eastern Hemlock, American Elm, Flowering Dogwood, Striped Maple, Mountain Ash, Red Oak and Mountain Laurel. CCC men were proud of such work; one man told Western Reserve University researcher Helen Walker that "Some day when those trees I planted grow large, I want to go back and look." Other former quarry land was leveled and grassed. One spring 1935 issue of the Camp Euclid newspaper, *The Surveyor,* exclaimed that a once badly-eroded quarry remnant near Bluestone Road now looked "ideal for bowling greens." The Quarry Picnic Area was dedicated in June 1936 in a South Euclid Kiwanis-sponsored ceremony which included speakers and music, and in which the enrollees of Camp Euclid and other CCC facilities took an active part.

Though the men of Camp Euclid left their park legacy in treasure sown and shaped, it was not all work and no play for enrollees. There was ample free time when enrollees both could relax and study.

Reading was one popular activity that both entertained and furthered educational goals at Camp Euclid and at CCC camps in general. Despite the limited formal educational backgrounds of most CCC enrollees, reading was a favorite pastime both at camp and before the men joined the CCC. Sources on the subject confirm these points. One has to understand that in the pre-television era, reading was more popular than it is today. The library in the Camp Euclid Recreation Hall was warmly welcomed upon its August 1935 completion.

When Lester Gallogly surveyed reading preferences at three unidentified Ohio camps (Camp Euclid possibly among them), he found that travel and adventure stories were popular. The most-perused camp library magazine categories were Western, sports and mechanical. The 2/9/1937 *Surveyor* reported holdings of 1000+ novels and 400 non-fiction books. That issue of the newspaper also stated that the crafter of adventure stories, Rafael Sabatini, as well as Western writers William McCleod Raine and James Hendryx, were favorite authors among Camp Euclid readers. (Raine was a graduate of nearby Oberlin College, a fact probably not known to the Camp Euclid men.)

Gallogly observed that the non-fiction books read by the men tended to be academic or vocational texts complementing the many classes held in camps. Both Gallogly and Western Reserve's Professor Walker found the instructional books in the camp libraries more consistent than the course work, which was dependent on the facilities on hand and the style and background of individual teachers.

Related to the interest in reading, at least three newspapers were published at Camp Euclid. The *Surveyor,* published from 1935-1937 (consulted for this essay), came out semi-monthly. While from time to time, the camp-written *Surveyor* bragged how favorably it compared to other area CCC papers—for example, its issues were generally longer than those in the *Kendallite,* a Summit County CCC camp paper—*The Surveyor* was specialized in its offerings. It gravitated to officer- and staff-written motivational essays and contrasting enrollee-submitted gossip and jokes. Other papers varied greatly. The *Kendallite,* for example, also a semi-monthly, had more practical tips on health, safety and employment than the *Surveyor* and also more updates on enrollees. As newspapers in general, both the *Surveyor* and *Kendallite* were heavily influenced by their editorship; changes in editorship at either paper brought swift and radical thematic changes.

Camp Euclid enrollees' love of reading perhaps made up for deprivations experienced earlier in life. CCC enrollees in the Ohio camps in the Gallogly study came from considerably worse living situations than average. These homes had few books, and only 35% took three or more magazines; 55% of them took none. Half of the surveyed CCC enrollees came from homes with only an outhouse, or a bathroom otherwise not in the home; less than a quarter had central heating; only 13.5% had a telephone.

From 1933 to 1937, Camp Euclid offered a footing in life for its vulnerable, impressionable young men, all 17-23 years in age. In this regard, Camp Euclid was one of myriad Junior Camps nationwide. In the middle of 1937, Camp Euclid was converted to a Veteran Camp, one of several as part of a popular and governmental movement to give greater support to Great War and Spanish-American War veterans, who felt forgotten. Enrollees since the CCC's 1933 inception had always included veterans. By the CCC's 1941 demise, 225,000 veterans had served in 150 nationwide camps just for them. In both 1938 and 1939, Camp Euclid was at full capacity of 200 veterans. The Veteran Camp continued through 1941. By that spring, enrollees were down to 175 because more men were departing for regular employment.

In 1944, new owners bought five Camp Euclid buildings and hauled them away, including the camp greenhouse. Today evidence of the Euclid Creek Park's industrious Depression-era residents can be seen in the many trails, bridges, stone retaining walls, thousands of transplanted trees, and more at Euclid Creek Reservation and other Cleveland Metroparks, such as North Chagrin.

Centennial

Notre Dame College

by Eileen Quinlan SND PhD

Barely five years after South Euclid incorporated as a village in 1917, Notre Dame College held its first classes seven miles away in a frame house off Superior Avenue in Cleveland. When the village was not quite nine years old, ground was broken for the first College building on the Green Road campus. In 1928, Notre Dame moved to its current location on College Road. In the succeeding years, South Euclid and Notre Dame have grown, struggled, and come to maturity in a neighborly partnership.

In Cleveland in 1920, a woman who wanted to work toward a bachelor's degree had one college choice: Flora Stone Mather College of Western Reserve University. So when the students at Notre Dame Academy at Ansel Road and Superior Avenue began to petition their teachers and principal for an opportunity to do college-level work in a Catholic setting, the wheels began turning that would make Notre Dame College a reality.

In the spring of 1921, conversations began with the general superior of the Sisters of Notre Dame, Bishop Joseph Schrembs of the Diocese of Cleveland, and the Ohio Department of Education. Plans were fast-tracked: the Sisters began developing curriculum, faculty were hired, marketing ideas were in place, a few Sisters were sent to pursue advanced academic degrees, and a wide-ranging search began for a suitable property on which to construct a college campus. When twenty-three young women began their freshman year on September 18, 1922, on the grounds of Notre Dame Academy, at the intersection of E. 93, Superior and Ansel Roads, the search had already led to farms in the Heights area.

Early in 1923, the Sisters found "an attractive site on Green Road, in South Euclid Village . . . approximately forty acres . . . practically level [with] three orchards and many large forest trees," as the community historian related. The property was leased from the Jordan family for $150,000 with an option to purchase. During the 1920s, the large farmhouse on the property was used as a residence for Sisters who needed to recuperate from illness in the fresh air of the countryside, away from the congested central city. As the Sisters of Notre Dame had also begun to teach in the new parish school at St. Gregory the Great, about a mile north on Green Road, the Sisters began to be a presence in South Euclid Village.

Exhaustive fundraising began, and the Sisters began to add to the Jordan farm by purchasing 57 residential lots on the newly-platted Golfway, Lawnway and College Roads adjacent to the farm, and by planting more fruit trees, grape vines, and a vegetable garden. By 1925, the Sisters hired the architectural firm of Thomas D. McLaughlin and Associates to design the campus buildings, which were planned to be both college and provincial center for the Sisters of Notre Dame in Cleveland. Ground was broken in the fall of 1926 for the Tudor Gothic main building. Financial constraints limited the construction to only two of the three wings; it would be more than thirty years until the west wing was completed.

The Administration Building, as it is known today, was ready for use in 1928. On the ground floor in the north wing was the gymnasium/auditorium. Above it was the library; on the second floor seven classrooms, and the third floor Christ the King Chapel with its stained glass windows and organ loft. On the fourth floor of the east wing were rooms for the resident students; the third floor held the main kitchen and the student dining room (now called The Great Room), as well as laboratories for home economics. Classrooms, music rooms, a little theater

Administration Building in 1928

and administrative offices occupied the first and second floors. When the building was complete, during the summer of 1928, trucks and moving vans brought the College's books, office equipment, desks, chairs, and dorm furnishings from Ansel Road, and classes began with 30 resident students, and other students commuting by car. During the late 1930s, the College administration negotiated with the Cleveland Railway Company (later the Cleveland Transit System) to run a bus directly to the campus, enabling more students to attend Notre Dame without having to walk a mile from Mayfield Road. With the start of the fall semester in 1940, city buses made eight daily runs to and from campus.

Enrollment grew slowly during the 1930's—these years were the peak of the Great Depression—but the farm on the property provided fruits, vegetables, chicken, pork, beef and milk for the students and the Sisters. When some students couldn't afford to pay tuition in cash, their fathers and brothers worked off some of the payments by building tennis courts on campus. Despite the financial struggles, in 1933 the Sisters of Notre Dame were able to buy out the lease on the property, guaranteeing the College a permanent home.

By 1931 growth was steady enough that enrollment finally exceeded 100 students, and two Sisters had earned doctoral degrees and joined the faculty, enabling Notre Dame College to earn regional accreditation through the North Central Association. Sister Mary Agnes Bosche was the College's Dean, supervising the academic programs as well as campus life. The students were busy with classes as well as forming clubs and producing a newspaper, literary magazine, choral concerts, dramatic performances, and discussion series on politics and world events. Many young women launched professional careers with degrees in education, business, French, and dietetics, while others continued with graduate studies, internships and law school.

As World War II engulfed the nation, Notre Dame responded to wartime needs by developing an accelerated program by which a student could earn her degree in three years and three summers of coursework. In another component of the war effort, from 1939 until 1950, the College offered what is today called an RN-to-BSN, enabling nurses with diplomas to earn a bachelor of science in nursing. Like all other citizens, the College community participated in blackout drills, sold and bought war bonds, and shared the rationing of food and fuel products.

With the close of World War II, college enrollment increased, and increased enrollment meant that a separate residence hall building was needed: Harks Hall was completed in 1955. Seven years later Providence Hall was added, doubling the number of students living on campus. In 1961 the west wing of the Administration Building was completed, a structural match to the east and north wings which was made possible when one of the 1926 contractors, Collinwood Shale Brick & Supply, custom-fired enough matching brick to complete the building. While the exterior matched the original Tudor Gothic style, the interior of the west wing boasted state-of-the art technology, particularly in the new laboratories for chemistry, biology, business and studio art. The meticulous and beautiful construction was honored in 1983 when the Administration Building was placed on the National Register of Historic Places.

During the 1960s the baby boomers reached college age: Notre Dame's 1960 enrollment of 341 students more than doubled to 721 eight years later. The expanded student body now had a third residence hall, Alumnae Hall (renamed Petersen Hall in 2003), as well as Connelly Center, with its kitchen, dining hall and student activity center, which opened in 1968. The Clara Fritzsche Library was completed in 1971, providing meeting rooms and study areas as well as a home for the 88,000 volumes of the print and media collection. The campus was taking shape as an active academic and residential community.

Teacher education has been a major emphasis from its beginning at Notre Dame College, as it has been for the Sisters of Notre Dame since their founding in 1850. For its first forty years, Notre Dame offered course work leading students to earn Ohio high school teaching licenses. The Ohio State Department of Education approved the College's certification program in special education in 1967, in elementary education in 1970, and in teaching students with learning disabilities and behavior disorders in 1979. Teacher preparation programs expanded to adult learners in 1994 when Notre Dame began offering education courses in late afternoon and evening hours through the Teacher Education Evening Licensure (TEEL) program, enabling adults with bachelor's degrees to change careers and enter the teaching profession. Other enhancements in the Education Division include the Ohio Board of Regents' approval of the Master's program in Education in 1991, the 2008 approval of a fully-online degree in education, and, since 2013, a master's degree in educational leadership for principals. This strong educational mission continues today, with many traditional-age and adult students working toward licensure for early childhood (P-3), middle childhood (4-9), young adult (grades 7-12), and multi-age as mild-moderate intervention specialists (special education).

Religious education to prepare teachers to serve in schools and parishes has always been a central ministry for the Sisters of Notre Dame. After Vatican Council II, the Center for Catechetics was established in 1972 to enrich the academic preparation of those who teach in parish- and school-based religious education programs for children and young people. When the Catholic Diocese of Cleveland launched its Diocesan Pastoral Ministry Program in 1981, Notre Dame offered the academic preparation in theology courses, including some in Spanish, while the Diocesan staff handled the spiritual formation of candidates. That partnership with the Diocese continued until 2016.

Adult women interested in resuming interrupted college careers or beginning their post-secondary education found a home at Notre Dame beginning in 1975 when lifelong learning opportunities, workshops and courses for credit and non-credit became available. The success of these programs led to the development of the Weekend College (WECO) in 1978. A WECO student could earn a bachelor's degree in four years by taking three courses each semester, with classes meeting on alternate weekends, Friday night, Saturday morning, and Saturday afternoon. In its 30+ year history, nearly 800 women earned degrees though the WECO program.

While some found weekend classes an attractive option, late 20th century advances in technology made online education available to more people. NDC offered its first online course in 1999 with Sr. Teresemarie McCloskey's "John Henry Newman's Theory of Knowledge." The Division of Professional Education led the way into online programming, offering fully-online coursework for licensure students at its satellite locations around Ohio; by 2008 all courses leading to licensure were available online. At that time the College brought on its first full-time Dean of Online and Nontraditional Education, and by 2009 general education courses were being offered both on-ground and online. By 2017, Notre Dame was offering fully-online bachelor's degrees in business, criminal justice, education, nursing and psychology, as well as master's programs in education, nursing, and national security and intelligence studies.

Notre Dame has pioneered many other academic initiatives through the years. During the 1970s, young women from Yavne Teachers' Seminary in Wickliffe, under the auspices of the rabbinical college Telshe Yeshiva, took their liberal arts and education courses at Notre Dame. At the same time, police officers from several jurisdictions studied at Notre Dame in the Law Enforcement Education Program (LEEP), sponsored by Notre Dame's sociology department, through which two dozen men earned associate degrees between 1975 and 1980. The current Master of Arts in National Security and Intelligence Studies, which debuted in 2011, mirrors the mission of the Department of Homeland Security. Notre Dame responded to the local nurse shortage by introducing its bachelor of science degree in nursing in 2006, a program which is now state- and regionally-accredited. Some students enter the program as registered nurses seeking a bachelor's degree, while others pursue a four-year academic and clinical program. An online master's in nursing education has been available since 2014.

Academic excellence at Notre Dame is reflected in many signature programs. The College's Honors Scholars program boasted more than forty students pursuing an honors diploma at Notre Dame in 2016-17. Excellence in science, technology and mathematics studies was a hallmark of Notre Dame when it was an all-women's college that launched many women into medicine and scientific research. Since 2012, Notre Dame has been part of the Choose Ohio First STEMM program (science, technology, engineering, mathematics, medicine). In the first five years of the program, more than forty students have participated in scholarship and research in biology, as well as sharing the STEMM living-learning community begun in 2016. The Academic Support Center for Students with Learning Differences has been providing supportive services to students with documented learning disabilities since 2005, enabling these students to succeed in regular college classrooms and in pre-professional internship programs. Notre Dame's nationally-recognized ASC is one of only three such collegiate programs in Ohio. About 150 students are enrolled in ASC services in any given academic year; in 2016, twenty-seven ASC students earned bachelor's degrees.

Talented high school students have been taking on-campus classes—especially calculus and English composition—at Notre Dame since the 1990s; in 1993, for instance, 26 high school students were enrolled. When the State of Ohio launched its dual enrollment program, Notre Dame responded in 2008 both by admitting highly-qualified secondary students to classes on campus, and by offering NDC courses on high school campuses. When two local Catholic high schools had to close, Notre Dame provided a dual-enrollment senior year to 29 Regina High School students in 2010-11, and to 23 St. Peter Chanel students in 2013-14. Those students completed their senior year together, earned their high school diplomas, and also earned as many as 32 transfer-ready college credits. In the 2017 spring semester, four area high schools were offering NDC credit courses in their buildings to 186 students. In addition, 18 high school students from seven school districts in Cuyahoga, Lake and Geauga counties were taking courses on NDC's campus, earning both high school and college credits under the College Credit Plus program.

Notre Dame College has long been engaged in Greater Cleveland's interfaith activities. As part of her graduate studies, Notre Dame alumna Maggie Kocevar '90 was interviewing Holocaust survivors for the Shoah Foundation. After her unexpected death, Notre Dame carried on her work by establishing the Tolerance Resource Center in 1997, promoting research, outreach and education on the Holocaust, anti-bias issues and diversity, and amassing an extensive collection of educational materials now housed in the Clara Fritzsche Library. Today the Abrahamic Center carries on the work by developing educational programs for the College and the Greater Cleveland community, fostering mutual respect among all peoples, and celebrating religious, racial and cultural diversity.

The Eleanor Malburg Eastern Churches Seminar is an annual fall gathering of Christians representing the Roman, Byzantine, and other Eastern Catholic rites as well as various Orthodox traditions. Clergy and laity gather for a Friday-Saturday series of presentations focused on a specific theme, such as icons, liturgical prayer, or the Scriptures. In collaboration with area churches, Notre Dame College has co-sponsored and hosted this ecumenical event since 1985, the oldest and one of only three such regular gatherings in the United States.

Other aspects of Notre Dame's outreach into the wider community date back decades. During the 1960s and 1970s, Notre Dame's students served the community by tutoring children at inner-city schools, collecting food and clothing for the needy, and writing letters to soldiers during the Viet Nam war. With the organization of a vibrant campus ministry program, students today volunteer locally with Garfield Memorial's after-school program, with the homework help programs at the South Euclid-Lyndhurst Library, and with senior citizens at Light of Hearts Villa in Bedford. Students also participate in spring break immersions with Habitat for Humanity, recently at work sites in Alabama, and in immersions in Guatemala, where students with nursing and performing arts skills engage a village community for a week each May.

Art in the Circle - 2012

The community is also welcome on Notre Dame's campus for a variety of events throughout the year. The College's annual Christmas Tree lighting ceremony in December is always open to the public, as are the band and choral concerts. Student theatrical productions and Mercury Theatre Company shows are staged throughout the year in Regina Auditorium. The summer band concerts at Notre Dame have been a fairly regular feature in the community since the 1978 launch of "Sunday in the Suburbs" (later called "Sunday at Notre Dame"), a series of Sunday evenings of family entertainment on the College's front lawn that continues to this day. Art exhibits in the Administration Building and the Clara Fritzsche Library, as well as poetry readings, lectures, and the Books that Change the World series have been bringing College and community members together for cultural enrichment for decades.

South Euclid's annual Memorial Day parade begins in the College's Green Road parking lot before marching to the War

Memorial at Anderson Road. With the opening of the Joseph H. Keller Center in 1987, members of the community have been welcome as members who enjoy the weight rooms and the pool, particularly the water exercise program. For nearly twenty years (1984-2002) the Tot Spot, located in Harks Hall, offered child care for the children of faculty, students, and the local community.

Governance at Notre Dame has been a process of steady development. In its earliest years, the superior of the Cleveland Sisters of Notre Dame was the College president with the day-to-day operations in the hands of the academic dean. In the early 1950s a board of advisors was convened, made up of local businessmen who advised the Sisters of Notre Dame who comprised the Board of Trustees. By 1955 it was clear that the College needed the attention of a full-time administrator, so Sister Mary Ralph Fahey, an experienced secondary school administrator, was appointed president. In 1990 the Board of Trustees was reorganized, made up of business and community leaders with Sisters of Notre Dame holding 20% of the seats and retaining sponsorship of the College while the Board was charged with responsibility for College operations.

The physical appearance of the campus changed markedly after 1950. The farm buildings facing Green Road yielded to progress with the construction of Regina High School for young women which opened in 1953, but the large white farmhouse remained, housing the family of August Siemer who would continue to tend the orchards and vineyards for another thirty years. Most of the orchard was cut down in 1986 because the trees—and Mr. Siemer—were aging; the farmhouse was burned by the Fire Department in 1997. Those acres of green space remained until 2013 when Mueller Field (on Green Road) and Normandy Field (on College Road) were completed, providing turf fields for football and soccer; renovated softball and baseball diamonds were also finished that summer.

Since the turn of the twenty-first century, other major changes have occurred at Notre Dame College. During the tenure of Dr. Anne Deming (1996-2003), the College began admitting men as full-time undergraduate students, and competitive athletic programs in the NAIA (National Association of Intercollegiate Athletics) flourished. Enrollment growth continued and reached an all-time high of 2281 students (full- and part-time, undergraduate and graduate) under the leadership of Dr. Andrew P. Roth (2003-14). In these years, increased enrollment led to the construction of two new residence halls and the purchase of the Regina High School building. In 2013 Notre Dame athletics transitioned to NCAA D-II competition (National Collegiate Athletic Association). Since the inauguration of Thomas Kruczek in 2014, Notre Dame continues to be a vibrant presence in the community. During the May 2016 commencement, the largest graduation in College history, 261 bachelor's degrees and 72 master's degrees were awarded. At the close of the 2015-16 academic year, nearly 1300 undergraduates were enrolled at Notre Dame, representing 23 nations, 40 states, and 67 of Ohio's 88 counties. With nearly 500 full- and part-time employees on the College payroll, Notre Dame is the largest single employer in South Euclid.

Campus & Farm in 1955

Campus in 2013

NDC is proud of its roots in South Euclid, and pleased to be an engaged member of the civic community. As it looks forward to its own centennial in 2022, Notre Dame College lives its mission as a Catholic college in the tradition of the Sisters of Notre Dame, educating a diverse population on the liberal arts for personal, professional and global responsibility—beginning right here on Green Road in the City of South Euclid.

The City Incinerator

by Janet Dreyer

When my husband and I bought our little bungalow on Bluestone Road in 1953, we had no idea that there was a big incinerator behind our backyard. It was summertime and the trees were in full leaf. We couldn't see beyond the hardwood lot. In 1953 each of the newly-built houses had an incinerator in the basement.

It didn't take long to figure things out as we noticed the smoke, although it never bothered us. The smoke seemed to stay in the woodlot. What we did notice was that, every once in a while, full flaming sheets of newspaper would sail out of the lot and eventually land on the ground. Then the fire trucks would park on Bluestone and several fire fighters would cut through our lots to get to the flames. Wearing water tanks on their backs, they quickly put out the fires. And so it went until the incinerator was finally shut down for good.

The neighborhood kids would play in the woods, even making a movie there. In fact. one of the previous Fire Captains was part of the "gang." (I remember that he used to climb in the trees and sing hymns.) One day when my son came home, he told me that I should go and look inside the incinerator. When I peeked in the window, I saw about 20 huge rats running around. One day I saw one in my yard and that did it for me.

My husband took an old galvanized tub and bent it to hold a Havahart trap. Because someone had once told me that rats loved wheat crackers and peanut butter, that is what I used for bait. I tied a rope on the handle of the trap. After a rat was caught, I held the rope and lowered the trap into the tub of water. It was not a fun thing to drown them. Norway rats are very large and feisty, and they carry many diseases. They hiss as loudly as a cat. One after another I got rid of 13 rats. To this day I check for rat tracks in the snow. So far I have not seen any more.

But my story doesn't end here. Last summer I spotted four turkey vultures in the woodlot, cleaning up a dead animal. Then they flew into my yard. They have a wing span of six feet and look like ancient birds. Crazy. So the big incinerator is gone but the vultures are the garbage disposers now.

I have seen enough deer to form a long parade to downtown. I have seen the gray fox climb a tree. I have seen a snowy owl swoop down and fly off with a small skunk. On Bluestone we have way too many raccoons. I think they have been living in the sewer for a long time. We have hawks, owls, opossums, and a coyote. Guess what? I think I live in a zoo and I hope to live here for a long time.

Update on the big old incinerator: A while ago the Fire Department wanted to use the area for training, but they learned that burning of refuse had been done on the ground next to the incinerator. When the soil was tested, it was found to be contaminated, so they were unable to use it.

Cedar Center in the 1940s - 1950s

by Chuck Lissauer

During the years up to and after my graduation from college in 1960, the commercial strip on Cedar Road between Fenwick and Warrensville Center Roads was "downtown" for parts of South Euclid and University Heights.

My first memories of the area date to just after World War II. There was a strip of stores on the University Heights side, built in the early 1940s with a smaller Guinta's Supermarket on the west end and a Cleveland Transit System bus turn-around on the east end. Most of the

South Euclid side was the William F. Rawlings golf driving range, a garden center and vacant land. (Fenwick Road on the South Euclid side was then called Rawlings Road). A Standard Oil station occupied the northwest corner of Cedar and Warrensville Roads.

In the late 1940s and early 1950s commercial facilities were built on the South Euclid side, and the University Heights side expanded on both ends, reaching around the corner and going south on Warrensville. The Mayflower Village Apartment complex was built on the site of the golf driving range. The strip was a vibrant commercial center where one could purchase groceries, bakery, clothing, shoes and household items. One could go bowling, take piano lessons, learn to dance, do your banking, go to the doctor or dentist or chiropractor, hairdresser or barber. There were dry cleaners, shoe repair, a library, a gas station, a car wash, restaurants and bars. One could still play golf east of Warrensville Center Road on the University Heights side.

There were also employment opportunities. Most of the proprietors were Clevelanders. I worked at Guinta's Supermarket, bowled at Cedar Center Lanes, bought model supplies at the Sportsmen's Den, and records at Art Newman's. I banked at Cleveland Trust Co., had my hair cut at Gus Camma's barbershop, quenched my thirst with 10 cent drafts of Michelob at the Cross Roads Tavern, took group lessons in Latin American dancing at Arthur Murray, and golfed at the University Heights Golf Club.

Whenever I discuss the old days at Cedar Center with contemporaries, the subject turns to food. First there were the bakeries, a carbohydrate wonderland, including Heights, Smayda's, Kaase's, Sanders, Davis, New York and Hough. (Fortunately, chocolate coconut bars are still with us!) Second were the restaurants, nothing that could be considered high-end, but the available dining was a selection of easy-on-the-pocketbook tastiness. My first memory of eating at Cedar Center was at Jak-Kraw, the clubhouse of the University Heights Golf Club (no cleats in the dining room), which occupied what is now the site of Macy's, University Square, Wiley Junior High School and other buildings. They toasted their hamburger buns like the Toddle House. Jak-Kraw was the only place where I've ever seen Hunting Valley Ginger Ale, which came in a pear-shaped bottle and looked like Vernor's. The other early place was Lenny's, located in a free-standing building at the corner of Cedar and Vernon. They served hamburger and fries in a basket with red-and-white checked paper on the bottom. Lenny's later moved into a small strip center in the same space.

After construction in the late 1940s, the South Euclid side had a number of restaurants. The first place I went to with my parents was

Benky's, a kosher-style delicatessen owned by the Benkovitz family. The décor included large plates and utensils on the walls with a sign that said "Eat, drink and be merry with Sam, Fan and Gary." Benky's served a sumptuous dish called "chicken in the pot." In the early 1950s they moved to the strip on Warrensville at Silsby Road. Up the street were three more delis: The Tasty Shop, Solomon's and later on, in the late 1950s, Corky and Lenny's, all purveyors of corned beef sandwiches and other delights.

A special treat (when my Dad was paying!) was Harvey's Bar-B-Q Restaurant, owned by the Sandler family. I would wash down the wonderful ribs and cole slaw with a Dr. Pepper. The only national chain restaurant at Cedar Center was Howard Johnson's, home of ice cream, fried clams and clam chowder. But it was gone by 1958. There was a branch of Mawby's, the famous Lee Road hamburger place. The grilled onions made that hamburger sandwich.

The first Chinese restaurant at Cedar Center was Young's, located on the University Heights side on Warrensville. In the early 1950s, the spot formerly occupied by Benky's became China Gate. They served what I consider the gold standard for American-style Cantonese food until a few years before the demolition of the original building. It is now a mostly carry-out on the South Euclid side. Their wonton soup is still unmatched anywhere.

Memories of Cedar Center of the late 1940s and the 1950s, whether shopping or dining, takes one back to a magical place. Now there is little remaining of that era that would trigger a memory except for the aromas of China Gate and the relocated Corky and Lenny's and Davis Bakery.

Centennial

Maymore Shopping Center

by Carole Prochaska Smith

The old Green Road School was still standing when the Prochaska family moved back to South Euclid after World War II. During the mid-1950s Walter Smith, Sr. bought the school property including two old school bus garages, which he used to construct a store. He and his wife, Beatrice, opened a business: May Green Paint and Wallpaper. They also purchased the brown 4-family house next door for their residence.

Also in the 1950s, stores were built on the north side of Mayfield Road extending to the east, including a grocery store (Mancuso's), Kresge Dime Store, a drug store, a florist shop, a furniture store and some others. The space behind them was paved to become a parking lot, eventually to encircle the paint store, the brown house, and a small building that was the office for weekly newspaper, the *South Euclid Messenger*. Messenger Court ran in front of it from Mayfield Rd into the parking lot.

Sometime in the 1960's, the Smith family purchased the stores east of Mancuso's grocery store and became responsible for maintaining the parking lot and access road between the Green and Mayfield Rd entrances. The landlord of a few little stores between Messenger Court and Cleveland Trust refused to pay even a small amount of upkeep for the right to have their customers use Messenger Court to get in and out of the parking lot, and to park on part of the Smith parking lot, so the Smiths constructed a chain link fence across the parking area that prevented all customers from going between the Green Road and Mayfield Road exits. This was a big story about the "Spite Fence" until some agreement was reached and the fence was taken down.

Over the years, the brown 4-family house was demolished as was the Hussong farmhouse at the north border of the parking lot on Green Road, where a Burger King was built. When Walter Smith Sr. passed away in the mid-60's, his wife Beatrice continued running the paint store until she retired and that store too was demolished.

Maymore in May 2017. Rightmost store (Blockbuster) was already demolished and replacement center started in the rear.

Over the years tenants on Mayfield Road included a large furniture store later replaced by Blockbuster video rental store, a hair solon, a florist shop, a CVS pharmacy (which later moved across to the south side of Mayfield Road), school uniform store, a clothing store, a Chinese buffet, pizza shops (including Poppy's Pizza, managed for several years by the youngest Smith brother, Gene), and a popular dollar store, Just a Buck, managed by the Cuyahoga County Board of Disabilities. Eventually when Mr. Mancuso retired and closed the grocery story, Marc's opened in the space. Within a few more years, Marc's extended into the former Cleveland Trust (later Ameritrust) space, making it the space for Marc's pharmacy. A bit of trivia: the huge bank vault wasn't removed. It was just dropped into the basement and remains there still unless it will be removed when that building is taken down in 2017.

The latest chapter for Maymore Center is the sale in 2016 of the stores from Marc's to the eastern end of the property by the Smith Family and Mr. Mancuso. The new owner/developer began the demolition of the original buff brick 1950s building and the construction of a new set of stores in the northeast corner of the parking lot. Marc's and several present tenants will more there. The area where the original stores sat will become parking visible from Mayfield Road.

Centennial

The Story of Warehouse Beverage

by Al, Mike and Paul Speyer

So many times over the years, we have heard people say, "I remember coming into your store when I was little and you gave me a pretzel." It would be interesting to know how many thousands of pretzels that would add up to today!

Our story started in 1940 when our dad, Adolph Speyer, realized his dream by opening his first store at 4434 Mayfield Road called Speyer's Creamery and Delicatessen. There he sold beverages such as beer, wine, and soda pop, along with cold cuts, cheeses, fresh bread and canned goods.

Dad also married our mom, Angela, the year he opened the store. Originally they rented an apartment across the street from the Delicatessen in a building that he would eventually own. Because they loved South Euclid, they decided to take up permanent residence and bought a home on Avondale Road where they raised the four of us: three boys and one girl.

In 1947, as their family was expanding, Adolph also wanted to enlarge his business. He rented a larger store on Garden Drive behind what used to be Bemis Florist. Here he sold just beverages. One of his salesmen told him his store looked like a warehouse and hence the name was changed to Warehouse Beverage.

In 1949, the Gulf Gas Station at 4364 Mayfield Road, at the corner of Sheffield Road, was up for sale. Adolph decided to purchase the building as it was a better location to attract customers. He added on to the building, remodeled it and opened the new store in 1950. Unfortunately, three years later the store was destroyed by a fire caused by the incinerator in the back room. Adolph did not let this upset his dream. He temporarily ran his business from his other beverage store in the shopping strip at Mayfield and Genesee Road while he rebuilt the Sheffield store. Shortly thereafter he sold the Genesee store. He also owned beverages stores in Willoughby and Warren, Ohio

Long hours were required to run the store so he recruited our mom and some of our uncles to assist him. Business was good and, as we grew old enough, each of us boys began to work at the store. When Al, the oldest, graduated from Brush in 1959, Dad asked him to run the store so he could continue his adventure in the real estate world, having acquired some other properties. In December of 1961, Dad passed away suddenly. Al stayed to manage the store for our mom. As brothers Mike and Paul grew old enough, they joined Al in the store full-time. We truly are a family business. This tradition extended to many of our kids who spent time working with us also.

These kids were labeled "bottle boys." Back in the day, pop and beer were sold in returnable bottles. The customers would bring their empties to us to get their deposit money back. Sorting the bottles so they could be returned to the right distributor took a lot of time. This job was so big that, over the years, we couldn't just fill it with family so we hired many kids from the area, some of whom are still in contact with us today. One even married into the family. We did progress with the times, giving girls an equal chance, and changing the job title to "bottle engineer."

We had a few other old-time services we used to offer, such as home delivery and in-house charge accounts. We have seen modern ways replace these, but we will never give up our commitment to customer service and the relationships we have developed over the years. Many of our customers are "regulars," and we learned about their families as they grew to know ours. The sales reps and delivery crews who make weekly stops became our friends also.

Because of our strong connection to the community, we also found it important to contribute to it. We have made countless donations to the schools, the city's safety forces, Little League teams and many others who needed our support.

Seventy-six years have passed since our dad opened the door and things are a bit different since we started working at Warehouse Beverage in our youth. Returnable bottles are long gone and the shelves are now filled with a large variety of craft beers, boutique wines and supplies to make both beer and wine. Though times have changed, we still hope you see us as that store with the three friendly brothers who always had a pretzel for you.

Centennial

Gentlemen's Grooming Barbershop

by Shironda S. Williams

Throughout history, a barbershop has been a place where you can enjoy a trim, shave, lineup, shampoo, facial and more. Established originally in North Randall, near Thistledown Race Track, Gentlemen's Grooming Barbershop relocated to South Euclid in 2013, bringing loyal clients with them, even from as far away as Elyria. The variety in shopping, eateries, banking and other businesses, all within a half mile of Warrensville Center Road, has allowed Gentlemen's Grooming Barbershop clientele to enjoy not only a haircut but also everything the city has to offer.

And who are the clients of Gentlemen's Grooming Barbershop? Seniors, students, old-timers and new clients, folks who appreciate using public transportation, folks who like to support small, locally-owned businesses, and folks who are glad for a quiet building and a soothing atmosphere.

Since July 2013, Gentlemen's Grooming Barbershop has become a solid presence in the city of South Euclid. Owner Shironda S. Williams directs Gentlemen's Grooming Barbershop, providing education as well as personal care services, for women and for men, including styling, answers and tips on grooming needs. The staff at Gentlemen's Grooming Barbershop caters to all hair textures by using clippers, shears and comb to honor the pattern of the hair with creativity and precision.

Gentlemen's Grooming Barbershop is more than a barbershop; it's a place where we discuss current events, enjoy the sounds of smooth jazz, relax, or just observe in comfortable quiet. Clients at this one-chair operation appreciate that there are no cell phone interruptions, allowing full attention and quality service at every visit. The shop offers rewards and incentives such as baby's first haircut and birthday promotions.

In the last four years, Ms. Williams' interactions with other business owners have provided new insights on developing Gentlemen's Grooming Barbershop into a premier location for men's and women's grooming. In the near future, Gentlemen's Grooming Barbershop members may be enjoying an educational magazine with tips, discounts, and connections to other assets in South Euclid.

Gentlemen's Grooming Barbershop
1481 Warrensville Center Road South Euclid, OH 44121
gentlemensgrooming@yahoo.com
"Quality service for quality men and women"

Our Recycling Committee

by Michael Barson

When the South Euclid Recycling Committee (SERC) was founded in 1987, Ray Fitzgerald was the president, and the organization had simple goals: to promote recycling within the City of South Euclid, to educate and advise South Euclid residents, city officials, businesses, and students about "reducing, re-using and recycling," and to foster practices in South Euclid to sustain and improve the environment.

The early work of lobbying the city to start collecting recyclable materials finally bore fruit in January 1990 when Mayor Arnold D'Amico announced the formation of a recycling program in the city of South Euclid "aimed at achieving the long-range benefits of preserving our natural resources." The first collections of plastic and glass containers and aluminum cans were done in drop-off recycling bins at Mayfield and Rushton Roads near Green. Because of complaints of bees, the bins were relocated in 1991 to the South Euclid Service Garage area on Green Road near Monticello.

The Ohio Department of Natural Resources awarded the City of South Euclid a Special Projects Grant of $16,945 early in 1991 to encourage litter collection and recycling. With assistance from city staff, the South Euclid Recycling Committee spent several months preparing the grant with assistance from City personnel.

Despite its accomplishments, Mayor D'Amico announced the cancellation of the recycling program in December 1991. The reaction was swift, with newspaper headlines reading "Recycling Program Canned" and articles quoting the mayor calling the recycling program "a waste." SERC President Mary Gerber began a full lobbying campaign to save the program. Just a week later, the mayor responded to public opinion and reversed his decision, reinstating the recycling program. That decision breathed new life into the South Euclid Recycling Committee, opening the door to fruitful years of ecological education and activism in the community.

In June 1992, the curbside "blue bag recycling" Pilot Program began, allowing residents to put recyclable plastic, glass, and metal items in any blue plastic bag for tree-lawn pickup by South Euclid staff. The SERC held community meetings to promote this program and to enlist residents to assist by distributing printed information to their neighbors. South Euclid began a city-wide bluebag recycling for collecting plastics, glass, metal, and phone books in March of 1993, with SERC providing blue bags to all new residents along with recycling information, to encourage participation. For several years, Waste Management managed South Euclid's recycling, until 2012 when Kimble took over curbside recycling, providing each household with both a trash bin and a full-size recycling bin to replace the use of blue bags. Plastics, glass, metal, and paper were comingled in the bin. Recycling volume more than doubled in South Euclid.

SERC began sponsoring "The Ecological Home Owner" programs in 2005 to educate residents about ecological concerns in maintaining their homes. A reusable South Euclid shopping bag was designed by SERC member and Councilwoman Jane Goodman in 2006; nearly 500 of the bags were sold at city events. SERC also held the first "Freecycle" event at which residents could bring usable unwanted items to a central location (Bexley Park) where people who needed or wanted the items could obtain them, free of charge. This event has been held annually for over ten years. The first electronics recycling drive ("eCycle") was held in 2010, and it too has become an annual event.

In August 1992 the SERC began promoting composting and reuse of organic materials by sponsoring a "Don't Bag It" contest to encourage residents to leave grass clippings on their lawn, in order to help reduce landfill waste. In addition, SERC held classes to encourage residents to compost and reduce landfill waste, promoted rain barrel use, and supported hazardous waste drop off.

Paper recycling was another SERC initiative. Committee volunteers helped residents unload their bags of newspapers at the South Euclid Service Garage. The first magazine recycling drive was held in 1995, with the Welcome Wagon distributing information packets and recycling bins in all three city parks. By 1998 the newspaper recycling was adapted to include magazines and junk mail; three years later, the city began curbside collection of newspapers and mixed papers.

Knowing the importance of educating youth for environmental responsibility, SERC has made it a priority to engage school children in the recycling efforts. SERC collaborated with South Euclid/Lyndhurst public schools in establishing Environmental Resource Libraries. Children participated in contests decorating paper grocery bags and tee-shirts with environmental designs. For several years, SERC awarded a $200 scholarship to a Brush High School senior who had participated in environmental activities and demonstrated a desire to continue promoting such activities. SERC has a high profile at Bexley Park, installing a recycling container at the Playground of Possibilities in 2008, and launching a Little Free Library box in 2015 to recycle children's books to new readers. In conjunction with the South Euclid Centennial Commission, SERC oversaw a Recycled Art Contest in 2017 in which entries consisted of at least 90% reused materials. Cash prizes went to the winners in each of three age categories, ranging from kindergarten to adult.

SERC has become a familiar presence at many community activities, including South Euclid Home Days and Rock the Block, Green Fest, the Memorial Day parade, and Harvest Fest, providing informational materials, banners, and give-aways of soy crayons and seed packets, recycled-plastic Frisbees, and handmade newspaper hats. SERC has earned several awards over the years, including a "Trash Oscar" in 2005 from the Cuyahoga County Solid Waste District, and a 2006 citation from Cuyahoga County for having the most improved recycling tonnage increase.

Over its lifetime, SERC has enjoyed strong leadership from its presidents Ray Fitzgerald, Donna Smith, Mary Gerber, Jean Nadeau, Madelyn Pollack, Dan Grossman and Melanie Kutnick. In addition, it has been pleased to collaborate with many local groups, including the South Euclid/Lyndhurst School District, South Euclid Kiwanis Club, local Boy Scout and Girl Scout troops, the Brush High School Key Club, the South Euclid Fire Department (especially promoting aluminum can recycling to benefit burn victims), and the South Euclid mayors and members of City Council.

Our Historical Society

by Bob McKimm

In 1966, the United States was in the middle of the Vietnam War. Locally, George Urban had been mayor of South Euclid almost 20 years. Realizing that South Euclid was approaching its 50th birthday—its golden jubilee—he and his wife Helen formed the South Euclid Historical Society.

Together they helped the city prepare a soft-cover book titled *Golden Jubilee: 1917-1967 South Euclid*, crediting, in particular, S. Bruce Lockwood (editor and publisher of the newspaper *South Euclid Citizen*) whose daughter had given them access to his source material. Also credited were the South Euclid Regional Library, Margaret Leist, and Helen Urban, but many say that it was Mrs. Urban who wrote almost all of the book.

In 1967 the Society incorporated as an organization whose purpose was "to compile, assemble and keep up to date, the history of the City of South Euclid, Ohio; to publish and distribute material on this subject; to receive funds by gift or bequest and to use such funds for the work of the Society. All assets of the corporation shall be dedicated to the literacy and educational purposes of this corporation during its existence." The original trustees were Helen Urban, Ray and Nettie Doehring, Paula Shaw, and Maynard F. Elliott. They committed themselves to learn, keep, and write about South Euclid's history.

Because so many items of historical value, in addition to paper records, had been donated to the Society's collection, in 1975 the trustees added an additional task to the Society's mission and articles of incorporation: "to assemble and display artifacts and records." The Society now needed a home to present these artifacts for public display. The South Euclid Regional Library, then located in the Telling Mansion, offered the Society the caretaker's cottage of the estate in 1977. All the Society needed to do was to paint the interior and install safety features for public occupancy, such as exit signs and a panic bar. However, the cost of these improvements was about $4000, and the Society had no money at the time, making this apparently simple solution a difficult problem. Somehow then-President Tony Palermo managed to raise the funds, and the Historical Society Museum became a reality.

SOUTH EUCLID HISTORICAL SOCIETY   CHARTER MEMBERS

Row 1 - Ray Doehring, Vice Pres.: Paula Shaw, Sec.: Maynard Elliott, Treas.: Nettie Doehring, Curator: Georgia Salinger.
Row 2 - Shirley Doehring, Virginia Newman, Mildred Shults, Marie Brott, Iva Hillen, Elsie Weigand, Margaret Leist, Ethel Albaugh.
Row 3 - Willard Shults, Albert Lindahl, Charles Lasch, Katherine Lindahl, John T. Mohr, Howard Hillen, Fred Geisheimer, Ross Albaugh.

In the last quarter of the twentieth century, all of the South Euclid-Lyndhurst elementary schools sent their third-grade classes to the museum for a local history field trip. Dividing the students into four groups, docents introduced them to all four major rooms in the museum within an hour. When the Great Recession made these field trips financially impossible, the curator of the Historical Society came to each classroom with her "museum in a suitcase" to introduce the children to local history. However, since the study of local history is not a direct match with state learning standards, these "museum in a suitcase" visits have not happened recently. The Society hopes to find new ways to bring children into contact with the history of their community.

The Historical Society's collection contains many items of interest, but few of significant street value. So when, near the turn of the century, someone broke in and took several objects from the museum, the South Euclid Police quickly identified a likely suspect. After he confessed, officers ferried him around the area to retrieve the items he'd sold. The Society then installed an alarm in the museum.

Around 2005, the Society established a website (SE-Lhistory.org) and developed a listing of e-mail addresses for member and visitor communication. Grants from the Legacy Village Fund of the Cleveland Foundation allowed for the purchase of a laptop computer and PastPefect software for small museums. Over several years, interns John L. Clark, Grace Gielink, Marsha Shear, Andrew Stewart, and Abbey Wolfe did the data entry that moved the Society's paper records into a searchable database, including many photos. These interns completed several other projects, such as migrating paper records to archival folders, creating search aids, assisting with grant applications, and documenting the street development in South Euclid. Other professional steps taken by the Historical Society include joining the Standards for Excellence Program (StEPS) of the American

Association of State and Local History (AASLH), and embarking on projects to bring The Historical Society's collection into compliance with best practices for 21st century museums. We are also active members of the Northeastern Ohio Inter-Museum Council. (northeastohiomuseums.org).

After several years of exploration, the Cuyahoga County Public Library decided in 2012 to move the South Euclid-Lyndhurst branch into a more modern facility. Although many, perhaps all, of the Historical Society's board and membership personally regretted this decision, the Society publicly expressed no opinion about the move. The Telling estate was sold to the Richard A. Barone Charitable Foundation, which decided to modify its main building to house the Museum of American Porcelain Art (MAPA).

Once he acquired the estate, Mr. Barone asked the Historical Society to remain on the historic property, and encouraged moving the museum to the Gatehouse, directly on Mayfield Road. Major costs for repairs and remodeling were partially offset by a Legacy Village Fund grant and a Neighborhood Beautification Grant obtained through One South Euclid. An internal major donor fund helped offset much of the rest of the costs. Now the Historical Society is ready to establish a more modern museum that will be useful for community activities as well as a setting to display local history.

No account of the South Euclid-Lyndhurst Historical Society would be complete without recognizing the many large and small contributions of the board, membership, and donors, especially those of the curator, Esther Eich (who has served in that role for over 30 years) and her husband Al Eich, who served as president of the Society for 12 years until 2013 when Bob McKimm accepted the position.

The Blossoming of the Garden Club

by Susan Gold, Vice President & Treasurer

"The Times They Are A-changin", a song written by Bob Dylan, reflected the turbulent 1960s. The first Garden Club of South Euclid, established in 1931, unfortunately didn't change with the times and eventually disappeared.

But in 1998, when Councilperson Chelly Tufts wanted residents to get more involved in the community, one outlet she proposed was getting gardeners to help with beautifying the city. So that year, Councilperson Tufts organized a new South Euclid Garden Club (SEGC). She felt so strongly about beautification that the first line in the new garden club's Mission Statement was about that principle.

The SEGC started out with five gardens: Princeton/Cambridge, Belvoir/Cedar, Mayfield/Brush, Rushton/Dean, and Greenview. Through the years, additional gardens were planted. At first, most of the gardens were planted with annuals, which provided a floral display for the entire summer. But the costs year after year to replace the annuals were constantly going up. So President Barbara Collins (2003-2006) proposed that the garden club start planting perennials. The perennials, with their limited blooming times, would be paired with some annuals for summer-long color. Up to this time, each garden site was organized by a stand-alone committee that had the freedom to choose whatever the individual committee wanted to plant.

Then in March, 2008, the garden club received the news that a landscape architect was being brought on board by the city to redesign the gardens. The garden club was told to completely stop working in the gardens.

Now the membership decided that the club needed to grow in a different direction. Participating in the Memorial Day Parade provided visibility but more was needed. The second principle in the Mission Statement, encouraging community spirit, needed to be cultivated. The club agreed to set up displays at various city-wide events to provide information about the garden club. Although Home Days, which the SEGC had attended with a fundraising booth, was, unfortunately, discontinued in 2005, the club persevered.

The SEGC started setting up a table at the spring and the fall garage sales held at the South Euclid Community Center. In 2013, the club voted to reprise the Green Elephant Plant Sale which had been part of Home Days. The sale would now be held at a member's home on South Green Road, providing visibility to passing street traffic. This proved to be a fundraising winner for the club.

Spring Fest was started in 2004 as a children's luncheon with assorted activities. The club participated by helping the children plant pansies in a decorated cup. Green Fest/Great Neighbors was held from 2007 to 2010, which highlighted environmentally-friendly organizations, and local businesses and community groups.

Harvest Fest began in 2012, celebrating the community gardens that had been established in the city and the fresh food that was grown in these gardens. This event provided another venue for the club to display the benefits of joining the club and to provide answers to any questions that the attendees might have had. Rock the Block, which replaced Home Days as a community-wide celebration in 2015, was another opportunity for the SEGC to promote itself.

Scholarships to Charles F. Brush High School horticultural tech graduates were granted beginning in 2007. These students attended the

Gates Mills Environmental Education Center, which was part of a consortium of tech programs that Brush participated in.

Decorating the South Euclid-Lyndhurst Library at the Telling Mansion during the winter holidays started in 2003. This provided a creative outlet for the club and provided an activity during the winter. Unfortunately, the Cuyahoga County Library Board of Directors decided to eliminate decorations at all of the library branches in 2016.

Not being able to contribute to any beautification projects bothered some club members. In 2008 the Garden Club donated funds to the Playground of Possibilities, and in 2010 they donated funds to the beautification of the Community Center. Some members started to volunteer at the Restorative Gardens at the Ronald McDonald House in Cleveland. But by 2012, since nothing had materialized at the various garden sites that the club had maintained, President Lisa Fain (2011-2014) proposed to resume tending the plantings at the Welcome Signs, sites which were in complete disrepair. Students from Notre Dame College helped the club members to revitalize the gardens.

OneSouthEuclid invited the garden club in 2012 to plant some green spaces at the new Quarry Park Community Garden. Some of the members helped to plant flower beds at various locations around Quarry Park North, and helped to plant a Butterfly/Pollinator Garden along one side of the Community Garden. The Pollinator Garden helped the community gardeners to increase their vegetable yields.

With all of the garden sites now under one committee, the list of additional and proposed gardens has increased. In 2017 the South Euclid Garden Club maintained gardens at Belvoir/Lancaster, Princeton/Cambridge, Monticello/Belvoir, Belvoir/Cedar, Mayfield/Brush, Rushton/Dean, Quarry Park North, Quarry Park

South, Bexley Park, and the Community Center, as well as school gardens at Rowland Elementary and Greenview Upper Elementary.

But Father Time had started to take its toll on the members. Seeing that some members could no longer participate in physical activities, the club strengthened the Program Committee offerings. Education became the third principle in the Mission Statement. Many different presentations were offered, providing an opportunity to enrich the members' mental expertise. Plant exchanges enabled members to share their abundance of flowers and their wealth of knowledge. Garden tours of nearby residences offered a chance to view hidden gems.

With participation in community groups such as PTA, Rotary, and garden clubs waning, all such groups have been under pressure to survive. Hopefully, dynamic new ideas will appear on the horizon and to help forge a bright future for the South Euclid Garden Club.

The First Baptist Church of South Euclid (FBCSE)

by Pastor Bruce McLaurin

In October 1965 a small congregation of seven families (Heights Baptist Chapel) purchased four and one-quarter acres of land in the northwest quadrant of South Euclid. In March 1966 the Heights Baptist Church was constituted as a Southern Baptist Convention-associated church. Groundbreaking service for the church's sanctuary took place in July 1968 at 835 Trebisky Road.

In December of 1984 the Heights Baptist Chapel merged with Mt. Calvary Baptist Church to form what is now the First Baptist Church of South Euclid under the pastorship of Rev. Waldo Burd.

On April 23, 1978, groundbreaking for an educational wing began. A parking lot and driveway were laid in the summer of 1981. Pastor Burd challenged the congregation to pay off the mortgage, which they did in 2000, while celebrating Pastor Burd's twenty-five years of faithful service.

Firtst Baptist Curch of South Euclid in May 2017

On the morning of July 30, 2001, a neighbor called the fire department to report a major fire in the church's educational wing.

Regretfully, the entire wing was destroyed. Rebuilding of the educational wing was completed in 2003.

First Baptist Church of South Euclid is a multicultural congregation, endeavoring to bring people to the saving grace of Christ Jesus and fellowship in His family; developing them to Christian maturity, and equipping them for their particular ministry in the body of Christ, in order to bring glory to God. To impact the surrounding communities, FBCSE has a passion for ministry to our youth and senior citizens.

It is our vision to place a community center, The Faith Walk Center, on the remaining acreage on our church property in order to establish an inclusionary multi-purpose center that will serve the intergenerational needs of the surrounding communities, a non-profit facility dedicated to ministering to the needs of all people. We desire to cooperate with local businesses, sports organizations, and ecumenical endeavors, to bless the community and give honor to God. "Whosoever will, let them come." Further information can be found at our website fbcse.org

The First Baptist Church of South Euclid is located at 835 Trebisky Road, just south of Monticello. Our worship services are as follows: Sundays 9:45am Sunday school; 11:00 am Worship; 5:30 AWANA; 6:00pm Worship. Wednesdays 6:30 pm Bible Study and Prayer Service. Our phone number is 216-381-1164. May the grace of God bless and keep you.

The Doll House

by Dale Ann Guidroz-Henderson

March 2017 marks my 20th year as a resident in South Euclid. Throughout this period I've experienced numerous changes in my neighborhood as well in my own personal growth. Looking back, I find it amusing to compare the fundamental differences in the critical thought processes between a 37-year- old woman versus the same woman twenty years later, but I am here to articulate the interesting ride it has been.

In March of 1997, exactly one year to the day of my first bout with cancer (there have been subsequent), I moved into my little house on Golfway Road. Having been long-time friends with a family on Maywood, I, like everyone else in town, would cut down Golfway regularly to and from Green Road, to points beyond. I remember always slowing down to look at the sad, tired little home with maroon shutters, as though it were reaching out to me in some subliminal way. Oddly, when it was ultimately listed for sale, I jumped at the chance to buy it because of the latent energy I felt had been "calling out" to me.

It became testament to one of life's lessons in honor of the old adage: *"beware of what you wish for."*

The little house was in awful shape. It had been a rental home for many years, and its neglect was tragically apparent. Technically, I knew all of this when I purchased the home, so when others questioned my wisdom, I arrogantly believed that working on a "fixer-upper" would be a positive learning experience. In addition, I internally reasoned my choice by comparing it to my long-time animal rescue advocacy efforts: I believed I was giving this home a "second chance." I compared my efforts to those of shelter animals who need to relearn trust, re-believe in love, and be provided supportive care. Ultimately, I was right, but like dogs and cats abused and neglected for so long, it was a tough road reaching the Holy Grail.

Three years and quite a bit of money (coupled with an enormous amount of dust) later, (including the construction of a front porch), the little tired house on Golfway Road was reborn into what many refer to now as "The Doll House." Decorations for changing seasons, and multiple landscape plantings have transformed what was once an eyesore into a home that the many dog walkers who travel past articulate it "makes them happy."

I grew up in a very connected neighborhood in New Jersey in the 1970s, an era before central air conditioning and online computer gaming dissolved human interaction. What I love about my neighborhood is that its longtime constituents seem to embrace the tenets of that period in history, by continuing the neighborly art of interaction and involvement. Although the expansion of the College has created some challenges to that sense of camaraderie, the overall vibe of the block remains connected. This belief was reinforced this summer, when my sister and her husband came to my home, and the first thing my sister said is how much my South Euclid neighborhood reminded her of our hometown in New Jersey. They live in the land of subdivisions and Home Owner Associations where they learn about their neighbors in a shared online newsletter.

I'm often reminded of the relationships my mother had when I was a child with our local support entities, like our pharmacist, the butcher, and the tailor. These relationships, founded on commerce, evolved into long lasting friendships well into their retirement years. To some extent, I feel as though her spirit lives through me in the long-time relationships I've developed in South Euclid. I'm not a big consumer, but I know I can always call Joe at Belvoir Pet Hospital, Sunny at South Euclid Humane, Yuri at Upholstery Talk, Mike on Maywood who works at Marshall's, and Keith at the City of South Euclid, who all know me by my first name. (For the record, I miss the menu and the people at the old Grande's Restaurant).

My husband, who moved into my house with me eight years ago, likewise has become involved with the City. As an architect, he designed the community enclosure for *One South Euclid* at the corner of Mayfield and Green Roads. In addition, between him and other urban farmer wannabees in the City (specifically South Euclid resident Dr. Laurel Tree, also part of the staff at Belvoir Pet Hospital), they created the "South Euclid Chickeneers". He and Dr. Tree were instrumental in helping the City design ordinances to enable humane and practical poultry farming within the city limits.

He has also been involved with the Warrendale Road Community Gardens for many years. (We're the plot with the cool weather hoops for kale, spinach, and lettuce for fall and spring planting.) We have marched in the Memorial Day Parade carrying signs for the

Community Garden Group, with seed packets proudly pinned to our hats. I became a Cuyahoga County Master Gardener a few years back, and have since become a "Mentor" to local gardeners for the Eastway Community Garden.

My husband and I expect to remain in South Euclid for several more years. However, as the College continues to expand, and our neighbors age out of their homes and move elsewhere, I expect we will at some point follow suit. However, because this house is the place where I have lived the longest in my 57 years on this planet, I will always remember the little "Doll House" on Golfway Road with a comforting smile.

And that smile will remain when I articulate to others that I will always consider South Euclid to be my home.

Notes

Notes for "South Euclid on the Portage Escarpment: Forces of Landscape Change"

1. James F. Pepper et al., 1954: Geology of the Bedford Shale and Berea Sandstone in the Appalachian Basin. *Geological Survey Professional Paper 259*. Plate 13E: Paleogeographic map of early Berea time (Figure 2, herein).

2. Charles S. Prosser, 1912: The Devonian and Mississippian Formations of Northeastern Ohio. *Geological Survey of Ohio, Fourth Series, Bulletin 15*.

3. Joseph T. Hannibal et al, 2007: The Euclid Bluestone of northeastern Ohio—quarrying history, petrology, and sedimentology. *Indian Geological Survey Occasional Paper 67*.

4. Jack C. Pashin and F.R. Ettensohn, 1995: Reevaluation of the Bedford-Berea sequence in Ohio and adjacent states–forced regression in a foreland basin. *Geological Society of America Special Paper 298*.

5. The Euclid bluestone is variable in color. It is usually light gray when freshly exposed. Nevertheless, exposures often weather (oxidize) to buff, brown or rust red. In the 1830s the grayness was described as blue, probably to distinguish the Euclid sandstone from the overlying buff-colored Berea Sandstone. With commercial quarrying during the 1870s, 'bluestone' became a trade name for the Euclid sandstone.

6. The action plans are prepared with aid from the Northeast Ohio Regional Sewer District, in conjunction with Bluestone Heights, Cuyahoga Soil and Water Conservation District, Doan Brook Watershed Partnership and the Friends of Euclid Creek.

Figure Captions for "South Euclid on the Portage Escarpment: Forces of Landscape Change"

1. South Euclid on the Portage Escarpment, regional view. USGS LiDAR elevation data.

2. 'Ages' for South Euclid landscape change. Read from bottom-up. Ma: million years ago; ka: thousand years ago; CE: Common Era.

3. Ohio Bay in the Appalachian foreland basin (Late Devonian Period). Pepper et al. Plate 13E.[1]

4. South Euclid on the Portage Escarpment, local view. USGS LiDAR elevation data. Sawmills: T. Addison (1812); T.J. Webb (~1830). Broken line: Lake Maumee shoreline. OG: Oakwood Green; LM: Langerdale Marsh.

5. Euclid Creek Welsh Woods cliff face, 1912. Prosser.[2]

6. Portage Escarpment north-south bedrock profile, approximately following Green Rd. Vertical scale exaggerated. The South Euclid surface rock sequence lies within the broken lines. At right, the numbers indicate elevation above sea level.

7. Euclid Falls and Bluestone village. USGS LiDAR elevation data. ERR: Euclid Railroad sidings. Broken line: filled-in area of the Nine Mile Creek gorge.

8. Cathedral Rock bluestone massif, 1953. Courtesy of Cleveland Public Library Photograph Collection.

9. Euclid Falls sandstone rock shelter, 2014. R. Larick.

10. NEORSD (lighter) and Euclid (darker) storm sewer service areas. Courtesy of NEORSD. *Major stormwater storage facilities*.

11. Langerdale Marsh wetland, 2016. Courtesy of Biohabitats.

12. Oakwood Green wetland, 2014. R. Larick.

Notes For "South Euclid in the Western Reserve: The Legacy of Euclid Township"

1. Roy Larick and Craig Semsel, *Euclid Township, 1796-1801: Protest in the Western Reserve*, 2003. WRHS Publication 191, Euclid Historical Society Publication 1.

2. Moses Cleaveland, personal diary, 1796. WRHS Mss. 104 Container 1 Folder 11.

3. Moses Cleaveland, contract with Seth Pease & others. WRHS Mss. 1 Roll 1 Folder 10.

4. Seth Pease, at a Meeting of the Proprietors of No. 8 in the 11th Range of Towns in New Connecticut held at the City of Cleaveland this 30th day of Sept. 1796. WRHS Mss. v.f. E relating to Euclid, O. Board of commissioners.

5. Wilma P. Stine (1937). "An Early History of Euclid Township, Ohio." B.A. Thesis, Mather College, Western Reserve University, Cleveland. Euclid History Museum Library.

6. Moses Warren, field notes. WRHS microfilm, Roll 1. The classical Greek mathematician Euclid is considered the inventor of geometry and therefore the "father" of the surveyors' craft. For several decades after the Revolutionary War, many new settlements appropriated Classical Greek place names as an appeal to ancient ideals government and culture. "Euclid" deviates from the norm in appealing to a Classical Greek personage rather than to a place.

7. Seth Pease, autograph diary and journals, 1795-1797 (transcripts). WRHS Mss. Roll 4 Folders 88, 89.

8. Between the Cuyahoga River and Nine Mile Creek, the effective distance is nine miles, if traveling along Superior Ave to Public Square, and eastward on Euclid Ave to the stream. The distance between the mouths of the Cuyahoga River and Nine Mile Creek is little more than 8 miles along the shoreline.

9. Charles Parker and Joseph Landon (1797). Field Notes of the Town of Euclid. No. 8 in the 11th Range. June 1797. WRHS Mss. v.f. E.

10. Turhand Kirtland, *Land Book*, 1799-1815. Kirtland-Morse family papers; WRHS Mss. 1463, Container 1, Folder 4. "Plan of Town 8 in the 11th Range, called Euclid." WRHS Mss. Maps, Bound Volume Maps 60-69, p. 62.

11. *Geauga Commissioners' Journal* Volume 1, p. 53 (March 1810). "At a meeting of the Commissioners of Geauga County March fourteenth, eighteen hundred and ten, It was ordered by the board, that all that part or tract of county lying west of the ninth range east of the twelfth range – and north of Township Number seven, be created into separate and incorporate Township by the Name of Euclid. To have and to enjoy all the privileges and immunities allowed by law to election districts. And that the citizens of said district do meet as the law directs on the first Monday of April next, at the house of Walter Strong, and then and there, proceed to elect such township officers as the law makes necessary." Champion, March 14th 1810. Attest: Abm Tappen, Cssr.

12. The Euclid Historical Society owns the *Euclid Records* which are on display at the Euclid History Museum, 21129 North St, Euclid 44117.

13. During the 1870s, geologists would name the region's rock for their best known exposures. The stone of the lower ridge was best seen at Euclid Creek in Tract 6. Among the various names applied, "Euclid bluestone" has had the widest use. Alternatively, the stone of the upper ridge was massively exposed in Berea, and became known as the Berea Sandstone.

14. Mary Emma Harris and Ruth Mills Robinson (1966). *The Proud History of Cleveland Heights*. Women's City Club of Cleveland Heights, p. 41.

15. *Euclid Records*, 1828. District No. 5. [South Euclid] (14 families): Benjamin Sawtill, Benjamin Sawtill, Jr., A. D. Slaght, Cyrus Gilbert, Josephus Hendershott, John Allaton, Samuel Ruple 2d, Lawrence Ruple, Isaac Husong, Abner Heston, John Goulden, William Ruple, Samuel W. Dille, John Cowel.

Figure Captions for "South Euclid in the Western Reserve: The Legacy of Euclid Township"

1. Euclid Township, Connecticut Western Reserve. Nine Mile Creek village: light circle; Euclid Creek village: dark circle. South Euclid center (Mayfield at Green): light square.

2. Charles Parker and Joseph Landon: Euclid Township Survey field notes frontispiece detail, June, 1797. Courtesy of Western Reserve Historical Society.

3. South Euclid topography and tracts. Sawmills: T. Addison (1812); T.J. Webb (~1830). Primary quarries: bluestone: squares; sandstone: triangles.

4. Geauga County Commissioners: Euclid Township charter, March 14, 1810. Courtesy of Geauga County Archives.

5. *Euclid Records* frontispiece, April 2, 1810. Courtesy of Euclid Historical Society.

6. *Cleveland Herald* classified advertisement, December 20, 1819.

Centennial

References

References for "Our First Visitors: American Indians"

Cuyahoga Valley National Park Site bulletins: *Land of Refuge*, and *Prehistoric Peoples*, written in early 2000s.

[Jones, Rebecca.] Hopewell Culture NHP, *People who Came Before: The Hopewell Culture Curriculum Guide*. U.S. Department of Interior, 1997.

Mann, Charles C. *1491: New Revelations of the Americas Before Columbus*. Alfred A. Knopf, 2005.

Potter, Martha A. *Ohio's Prehistoric Peoples*. Ohio Historical Society, 1968.

References for "Euclid Creek Reservation and the Civilian Conservation Corps"

newspapers:

Camp Euclid Surveyor. 1935-1937. [semi-weekly] free, downloadable files at https://dds.crl.edu/crldelivery/21281.

Kendallite. July-Sept., 1935 [semi-weekly] free, downloadable files at https://dds.crl.edu/crldelivery/21119.

O'Brien, Dr. M.A. Informal progress reports. *Euclid Sun Journal*. 1938. [irregular] free, downloadable files at website of Euclid Public Library.

books and journals:

Bindas, K., ed. *The Civilian Conservation Corps and the Construction of Virginia Kendall*. Kent, OH: KSU Press, 2013.

Federal Writers' Project of the WPA. *CCC in Ohio*. ca. 1937.

Gallogly, Lester Harold. *A Study of the Personnel and Educational Program of Three Civilian Conservation Corps Camps*. MA Thesis. Ohio State University, 1936.

Centennial

Hannibal, J.T. et al. *The Bluestone of Northeast Ohio*. Indiana Geological Survey occasional paper. See https://www.cmnh.org/CMNH/media/CMNH_Media/C-R%20Docs/Invertebrate-Paleontology-Euclid-Bluestone.pdf.

Walker, Helen. *The CCC through ... 272 Boys ... Group Study of Cleveland Boys ...* : WRU Press, 1938.

archival:

oral history interview with Newton Bishop Drury. Truman Presidential Library. Independence, MO. 1972. Available at https://www.trumanlibrary.org/oralhist/druryn.htm.

YMCA. *Annual Reports*. 1917-1924. YMCA Records series I. Central Y files. Box 16, Folders 1-4: Western Reserve Historical Society. Cleveland., OH.

Cleveland Metropolitan Park District. *Annual Reports*. 1918-1951.